"I know firsthand that Jon Levy understands a lot about human behavior—he got me and a bunch of other busy professionals to cook him dinner. From his research and long experience, Jon is a master of building connections between people and enriching their lives in the process. This book explains, simply and engagingly, how he does it."

—Eric Maskin, Nobel laureate and economist

"I had no idea what to expect as I walked into a stranger's house with a bottle of wine. The beauty of the experience was in the simplicity of it all. It wasn't extravagant or pretentious; instead, it was a group of strangers cooking together. By the end we were all chatting like old friends. That's what this book illustrates so beautifully: life is about the people we surround ourselves with. Now I am borderline obsessed with the connections I have in my own life along with the connections in others' lives that led them to where they are today."

—Nathan Adrian, eight-time Olympic medalist, Team USA

"Normally when a strange man invites me to dinner in a strange home, I decline. But I, like all of my dinner mates that evening, was inspired by Jon's unslakable curiosity about humans and how we form bonds. It is in the pursuit of those answers that Jon is able to set the table scientifically, mentally, and, of course, literally, for strangers to engage in thoughtful, meaningful, and, in many cases, life-altering conversations. Explained in these pages are the how and why connecting with fascinating strangers is so important. This book is as close as one can get to actually attending one of his extraordinary dinners."

—Iliza Shlesinger, comedian and actress

"I grew up in a close community of cousins who built my confidence through love, humor, and food. As an adult, I wasn't pleased that twenty-seven Greeks couldn't come with me to Hollywood events and laugh at my jokes. Isolation is no fun. Making burritos at an Influencer's dinner is. This book will make you as confident and good looking as your mother says you are."

—Nia Vardalos, Academy Award–nominated actor
and screenwriter, *My Big Fat Greek Wedding*

"Jon and his dinners are focused on bringing people together under the umbrella of unique experiences to share a love of life and the spirit of connection."

—Jesse Carmichael, Maroon 5 guitarist

You're Invited

Also by Jon Levy

The 2 AM Principle

You're Invited

THE ART AND SCIENCE OF CULTIVATING INFLUENCE

Jon Levy

HARPER
BUSINESS

An Imprint of HarperCollins*Publishers*

HarperCollins books may be purchased for educational, business, or sales promotional use. For information, please email the Special Markets Department at SPsales@harpercollins.com.

FIRST EDITION

Library of Congress Cataloging-in-Publication Data
Names: Levy, Jon (Behavior scientist), author.
Title: You're invited : the art and science of cultivating influence / Jon Levy.
Identifiers: LCCN 2021002177 | ISBN 9780063030978 (hardcover) | ISBN 9780063030985 (ebook)
Subjects: LCSH: Social influence. | Persuasion (Psychology)
Classification: LCC HM1176 .L48 2021 | DDC 302/.13—dc23
LC record available at https://lccn.loc.gov/2021002177

21 22 23 24 25 LSC 10 9 8 7 6 5 4 3 2 1

To the love of my life,
you are my star,
you are my fire.

To all those who have cooked me dinner.
I have known no greater privilege than sharing moderately edible
meals with you and having washed dishes together.

Contents

_____

Part I

The Influence Equation

Chapter 1

The Power of an Invitation

———

It was the fall of 1961 and Jean Nidetch was having what she called a "thin day." At five foot seven and 214 pounds, the thirty-eight-year-old self-described housewife from Queens, New York, was, by her view, the view of her neighbors, and the view of practically everyone other than her loving husband, overweight. Dressed in a size 44 muumuu that she relabeled a size 20 in an effort to make herself feel better about her proportions, she went to the supermarket to pick up groceries. As she checked out, she felt the need to assure the clerk that all the boxes of cookies were for her kids, but the truth was that Jean would hide them in the bathroom, where she would binge eat entire boxes at night. As she strolled the supermarket aisles, an acquaintance complimented her on how great she looked. Jean welcomed the kind words, and then the woman added: "When are you due?" Jean was mortified—the woman thought she was pregnant. When she got home, she looked in the mirror and promised herself to use those words as motivation to finally lose the weight. Jean believed that through self-control and determination alone, she would achieve her goal. She was wrong.

Anyone who has ever committed to a weight loss diet knows that hard work and self-control just aren't enough. Jean had tried every outlandish plan to reach a healthy weight, from eating nothing but eggs or grapefruit, to starvation, to the latest celebrity fad she would read about in a magazine. She would always be able to knock off a few pounds, but the moment she reached for her favorite foods, she would overindulge, and the pounds would come back, often with a few extra. After years of this she realized that if she was going to lose the weight and keep it off, she needed a different approach. One year later Jean had lost seventy-two pounds, but what was truly exceptional is that over the next fifty-three years not only would she keep them off but she would help tens of millions of people around the world lose hundreds of millions of pounds, likely saving countless lives. In the process Jean Nidetch became a multimillionaire and an international celebrity, all in an era when her credit cards still said Mrs. Marty Nidetch. If you have ever heard of Weight Watchers International, it's because Jean understood the importance of human connection and the community effect.

While Jean was an overweight housewife looking to get healthier, Frederick Bailey's story couldn't have been more different. Though the stories are separated by over 120 years and are incomparable in their challenges and motivations, on closer examination you can see an incredibly powerful connection between the two. It was September 3, 1838, and to say that Frederick was anxious would be an understatement. As an escaped slave, he knew his life was on the line. If he were caught, he would be tortured, possibly shot, or torn apart by vicious dogs to be made an example of.

His plan was to avoid being noticed by jumping on the train just as it was leaving the station from Baltimore, Maryland, a slave state, to Philadelphia, Pennsylvania, a free state. Once on board, he would sit segregated with the other Black passengers in the "negro car." He hoped that the jostle of the train and the busyness on board would prevent the conductor from noticing the discrepancies in his papers. This would be assuming he wasn't recognized by someone and captured or arrested at the border. To fool the conductor, Frederick managed to secure borrowed papers from a local free sailor, and to play the part, he dressed in sailor style with a red shirt, hat, and cravat.[1] If he was lucky, the combination of papers, outfit, and his knowledge of ships (he was forced to work at a shipyard for some time) would be enough to throw off suspicion. When the conductor came, Frederick passed him papers with a prominent seal on them to demonstrate their authenticity. With hardly a look, the conductor moved on, and

Frederick had made it through his first challenge. Over the next day he would go from train to ferry, to train, to steamboat landing at Philadelphia. At each port, he avoided the possibility of police or bounty capture and the numerous men who, with a long enough glance, would recognize him. After arriving in Philadelphia, he boarded one last train to New York, and by the next morning, he was a free man.

Three years later, Frederick, now going by the last name Douglass to avoid recapture, accepted an invitation to attend a meeting of the American Anti-Slavery Society (AASS). It was hosted by William Lloyd Garrison, the publisher of the abolitionist paper the *Liberator* and cofounder of the organization.[2] Douglass was invited to share his story with the crowd. When Garrison heard Douglass's words, he immediately knew that Douglass could become an important figure in the movement. What Douglass could have never predicted that day was that thanks to the Influence Equation and the power of an invitation, two ideas we will explore in detail, his public speaking and writing would play a critical role in the movement to end slavery, the election of Abraham Lincoln, and the freedom he and his fellow Black men, women, and children deserved.

Jean's goal and the abolitionists' goals were clearly different, which is why I chose their stories. They were separated not only by more than a century but also by race, religion, culture, and objectives. Jean was committed to the very personal struggle of helping people of all walks of life find health. After all, at least 2.8 million people die due to obesity-related issues every year.[3] And the abolitionists were fighting for the social and moral obligation to give freedom and equality to humans in bondage. Even though their journeys and missions were incredibly different, what led them to succeed was the same thing: they found a way to bring people together and create deep and meaningful connections between them.

I came to realize the importance of creating meaningful relationships through a very personal journey. By my late twenties, I had mounting debt and a failed startup, I was overweight, and I was struggling in the greatest economic downturn we had seen in more than a half century. I had become the poster child for "Not living up to his potential."

Fortunately, I was able to piece together what Jean realized in her weight loss program and the strategy the AASS used to spread their message looking at scientific research. I examined studies on human behavior, neuroscience, economics, and decision making in hopes of developing personal and career success, and for me, the results were life changing. In fact, it was so compelling, it led to a career as a behavioral scientist, consultant, and researcher. What I did with these insights was strange to say the least. I convinced complete strangers, many of them among the most influential people across various industries, to cook me dinner. Over the course of a decade, this dinner developed into what many consider to be the most exclusive dining experience in the world.

We host twelve strangers at a time, but there's a catch. Not only do the guests cook the meal together but, as they do, they can't talk about their careers or even give their last names. Once seated to eat, attendees discover their fellow guests are all industry leaders, from Nobel laureates, celebrities, and Olympic medalists to award-winning musicians, artists, and even the occasional member of a royal family. This experience became known as the Influencers Dinner because of the ability of its participants to influence their industries. As participants bonded at dinners, cultural events, and reunions, the Influencers community developed the mission to positively impact each other, our communities, and hopefully the world. Since its inception, I have hosted thousands of people across hundreds of dinners and developed a consulting firm that works with many of the world's biggest organizations to help them connect with their employees and most important customers in deep and meaningful ways. We have created private communities for tech brands and healthier company cultures for consumer-packaged goods companies. We have reimagined sales processes for startups by focusing on developing meaningful and lasting relationships with customers, and supported nonprofits in creating cohorts of donors who are loyal to the cause. Every dinner, event, and project I work on reaffirms a single universal idea for success that I learned in a seminar at the age of twenty-eight:

The fundamental element that defines the quality of our lives is the people we surround ourselves with, and the conversations we have with them.

Until I heard those words, I had been trying to improve my life by using strategies from every personal development/business book or class I could afford, hoping that they would fix the things that I thought were wrong with me. My life improved, but it was exhausting, and I spent my twenties beating myself up for not being rich, not having a perfect body, and not having an ideal relationship. Instead of insecurity and failure, I wanted the ability to produce extraordinary results and engage with people I thought were important. After all, those who are important to my success could be irrelevant to yours. In short, I wanted influence. I'm not talking social media influence—that didn't really exist back then and, frankly, I don't eat avocado toast and I look terrible in a bikini, so I don't think I'm suited for that career. I'm talking about the ability to influence my career and income. I also wanted the respect of business leaders, the ability to impact a social cause I cared about, and to have a healthy lifestyle.

If this seminar leader was right, there was a much easier way to influence the direction of my life. I needed to surround myself with people who had the characteristics I admired. Instead of setting a 6:00 a.m. alarm to go to the gym, maybe I just needed to make friends with athletes and fitness enthusiasts, then exercise would be part of my lifestyle. Instead of trying to stick to a budget, if I had friends who were experts at business, I would understand how to earn more and have the connections to find a better job. After all, making friends with people I respect and admire sounds a lot more appealing than hitting snooze four times and feeling bad I missed a workout or getting credit card late charges.

Jean eventually took this very approach. In time, she would surround herself with people committed to the same goals, but it took another experience for her to realize how much she needed others. Soon after she was confused for being pregnant, she heard about a free obesity clinic in Manhattan that was part of the New York Department of Health. After two buses and a train ride, she sat quietly in a room full of women looking to lose weight, listening to a slim and stern nutritionist she called Ms. Jones. To Jean, this woman was someone who had no empathy—she could never understand what it is to struggle with weight. Ms. Jones could never relate to the feelings of shame and sadness and the constant battle not to indulge. When Jean weighed in at 214 pounds, Ms. Jones assigned her a goal weight of 142 pounds. Jean was in shock—this was far less than she had ever weighed in her adult life. Ms. Jones stipulated that Jean would only eat the foods instructed, and nothing else.[4]

After ten weeks, Jean had lost twenty pounds. She was ecstatic with the results, but the weight-loss process was clinical and conversations between the participants wasn't encouraged, leaving her feeling isolated and yearning for someone to relate to. If she was going to continue to lose weight and keep it off, she needed a better support system, one that encouraged openly discussing her struggle. So Jean did something unprecedented. She extended an invitation to her friends she knew were struggling with their weight to come to her house for an evening of mah-jongg. Six women showed under the guise of a game, but Jean's real invitation was to a safe space for them to open up about their struggles with weight loss. As the evening unfolded, they shared their compulsive, unhealthy habits and their shames, and as they did, they began to feel liberated. It was the first time any of them spoke openly about their weight, all because of a simple invitation. One of the guests suggested they meet the next week, which Jean turned into every week. Meeting after meeting, her friends invited friends, and their friends invited friends, and within two months, her group had turned into forty women now meeting twice a week.

Jean was transparent about her lack of credentials. She wasn't a medical professional, just a housewife from Queens, but the advice of doctors wasn't working for these women anyway. What they needed was the incredible sense of community that is created when people can finally be honest about their struggle. The magazines Jean had been reading suggested that life could be a perfect dream with some simple solution, but for those of us living in reality, life is much more complex. We all struggle with something, whether it's anxiety from work, the isolation of depression, the fear of poor health, feeling like a failure as I did, or something else uniquely yours. The difference between us needing to pop a Xanax, overeating, or hiding our problems and us finding a solution is our relationships. This was the beauty of Jean's group. Jean provided a space for people to connect with one another, feel safe, build trust quickly, and in turn support one another. In that lies the strength of the community effect:

Our results are amplified when our relationships share a sense of community.

It seemed that Jean was proving my seminar leader right. These same women, pretending everything was fine, probably would have spent their time socializing around food, but Jean designed an experience that changed the context and turned the conversation to health. The consistency of running her gatherings twice a week led these women to form a shared sense of community around their weight issues. Instead of enabling unhealthy habits they became a nonjudgmental support system. Everyone who attended benefited from new friendships, habits, ideas, and routines.

It was at one of these meetings where Jean met Albert and Felice Lippert, a couple so plump they described themselves as beach balls. After four months of weekly meetings, Albert was down forty pounds and Felice almost fifty. They believed that the success of Jean's experiences could be franchised, with Jean as the public face of the company. After incorporating Weight Watchers International, they held their first official meeting on May 15, 1963. Over four hundred people showed up to a space intended for fifty. Six short years later, the franchises that Albert dreamed up were growing and the participants were shrinking to the tune of seventeen million pounds lost. In 1973, Jean and the Lipperts celebrated their ten-year anniversary at New York City's Madison Square Garden with a sold-out crowd of Weight Watchers enthusiasts. They had a lot to be proud of: the company had grown to 110 franchises and $15 million in annual revenue. By 1978, just fifteen years after its founding, the company sold for $71 million (the equivalent of about $280 million today) to famed ketchup company H. J. Heinz.[5]

Clearly an approach for success built on human connection makes sense. We can all think of stories of how human connection made the difference for personal, social, and business challenges, but after all my failed attempts to change my life, I wanted more than inspiring stories. I wanted evidence that focusing on developing personal connections would actually work, and for me, the proof came from scientific research that would have been no surprise to Jean.

By the 2000s, the obesity epidemic in America had reached a new high, and two researchers, Nicholas Christakis and James Fowler, asked a question: Is obesity the type of epidemic that spreads from person to person like a cold or is it a personal experience brought on by other factors such as genes and habits? The answer changed our fundamental understanding of human relationships.

Looking at thirty-two years of data across communities, they discovered that if you have an obese friend, your chances of obesity increase by 45 percent, your friends who don't know the person have a 20 percent increased chance, and their friends' chances go up by 5 percent.[6] We each have an effect three degrees out, and this kind of effect is also true for happiness, marriage and divorce rates, smoking, and voting habits, among other factors. Our lives are a by-product not only of our five closest friends, as people like to say, but also of our extended community.

Based on their research, you would think that bringing women who struggle with their weight together would make them more likely to gain weight, but instead Jean created a uniquely formatted experience for her community to change their conversation. Instead of spreading unhealthy habits, they focused on support. The same way word of Jean's invitations spread from person to person, so did new habits, ideas, and the feelings of belonging and acceptance. This is one of the reasons community-based organizations are so effective.

So, if habits, behaviors, and emotions are so contagious, one of the most important things we can do is surround ourselves with people who share the values or traits we admire. Through proximity, we can gain that trait. But we shouldn't just stop there. By introducing these people to one another, everyone could positively influence the group, and as their lives improve, ours would transform even more.

This idea was at the heart of Garrison's strategy for the abolitionist movement. It was not enough to reach people with his newspaper—he needed to invite them to come together, bond them around a cause, and empower them to take action by recruiting more people and pushing politicians to change laws.

To do this, Garrison and his fellow abolitionists started a lecturing agency system that sent representatives to towns across the North.[7] Speakers, who at times risked their lives facing violent pro-slavery mobs, would present ideas and share stories to illustrate how slavery was fundamentally opposed to the Christian ideals of the time. Invitations spread, bringing people together to bond and speak openly about the injustices of slavery. Participants were then invited to open local chapters, further spreading the message. Cities across the North began to host everything from local meetings to annual conferences. As a result, support grew exponentially. It is estimated that in the three years from 1835 to 1838 alone, the United States went from 225 abolitionist and anti-slavery societies to over 1000, with 250,000 members.[8]

When Garrison experienced Douglass's incredible ability to move the crowd at an AASS meeting, Garrison knew there was a unique opportunity for the movement. Douglass represented what pro-slavery advocates feared most—an example of an escaped, literate slave who could speak so emotionally that no good-hearted person could ignore the evils being committed. Douglass was invited to be a speaker for the AASS and traveled the North from meeting to meeting, winning hearts and minds. Both in talks and his autobiography, he revealed at great personal risk that he was an escaped slave. He described his enslaved life of abuse and torture in vivid detail. The book became a best seller and is still widely read today. Until that point, almost all the knowledge Northerners had about slavery was shared by Southern slave owners who presented the practice as kind and paternal. No one who read Douglass's account or heard him speak could claim slavery was kind.

As more abolitionist and anti-slavery societies were created and their influence spread, public sentiment changed. Historian Manisha Sinha points out that it was this abolitionist community structure that spread the cause across America. Abolitionist agitation paved the way for the rise of the anti-slavery Republican party of the 1850s and the election of Lincoln as president. They pressured President Lincoln to move on abolition during the war, resulting in Lincoln issuing the Emancipation Proclamation, which led to the end of slavery.

Regardless of what we want to accomplish, from affecting our habits, to championing a social cause, or even building a successful career or company, we can't do it alone. Bringing people together in a unique way produces contagious results. Ultimately, the people around you matter. Who you surround yourself with defines your success (whatever that means for you personally) and has the potential to change the direction of your life and our society.

That's what this book is about:

**The most universal strategy for success is creating meaning-
ful connections with those who can impact you, your life,
and the things you care about.**

There are a lot of theories on how to have a great life and accomplish what we want for our career, company, cause, or habits. But for
something to work for all of us it shouldn't require a college degree,
extreme wealth, or coming from the "right family." Instead, it needs
to be built on what we all have in common—what is at the core of
who we are as people—and how we behave and interact. Nothing is
more universal than our need to connect; it is what has allowed us to
survive as a species. We aren't loners like tigers or sea turtles. Every one
of us needs social interaction.

This is what made Jean so extraordinary. She didn't just give
women a diet plan; she gave them a way to congregate and connect,
forever changing the way they would relate to their health. Similarly,
the abolitionists brought people together, shared ideas, changed their
opinions, and empowered them to start their own groups and newspapers. In the process, they reshaped the course of America's future.
Their approaches were brilliant.

Notice that even though history remembers Jean and the abolitionists as significant figures, when they started their journeys there
was not a shred of evidence any of them would succeed. Jean didn't
know celebrities or the famous doctors; she was, in her own words,
an FFH (formerly fat housewife), and in the 1960s being a housewife
meant she still had to get her husband to sign the lease on her first
office. Meanwhile, Garrison and escaped slaves like Douglass, Harriet
Tubman, Sojourner Truth, and Henry Box Brown weren't wealthy
or influential businesspeople or elected officials. They had no real
power, but that didn't matter. Instead, they accomplished their goals
by inviting people to come together and creating a safe space for them
to learn and hear the truth.

Jean and the abolitionists didn't start their journeys knowing
prominent leaders, politicians, or celebrities. Instead their influence

was gained meeting by meeting over the course of years, but as their reputations grew so did their ability to connect with those who could have even greater impact. In fact, during the Civil War, Douglass showed up at the White House unannounced and within a few minutes met with President Lincoln,[9] and Jean shared the stage at her ten-year anniversary celebration at Madison Square Garden with a slew of celebrities and other influential people. You might think these kinds of results are limited to larger-than-life figures, but it actually doesn't matter if you are a wild extrovert like Jean or a quiet introvert who prefers the company of a great book like this one to being on a stage. While extroverts may be more apt to connect with many people, introverts are often better at creating deeper and more meaningful relationships. In this book, we will focus on the approach that works for your personality and what you care about.

The abolitionists and Jean teach us the lesson that our lives are defined by the people we surround ourselves with, not only because their behaviors and habits are contagious, but because when there is a profound level of trust and a sense of community, we can achieve what's important to us. This is the Influence Equation: our influence is a by-product of who we are connected to, how much they trust us in that capacity, and the sense of community we share.

Influence = (Connection x Trust) $^{\text{Sense of Community}}$

Once I realized that, I dedicated myself to answering three questions:

1. *What causes people to connect?* How do we get someone's attention so they want to engage with us?

2. *What leads us to build trust quickly?* The more important a person is, the less time we will have; how do we develop a deep and meaningful relationship quickly?

3. *What gives people a sense of community?* Why do you feel a kinship with some people you have never met before, and how do we foster that kinship toward a common goal?

To answer these questions, the first thing I had to understand was that connection is not networking. When we think of networking, we imagine a charismatic person who is artfully and effortlessly chatting people up and adding them on LinkedIn. If you have that type of personality, networking can be a great strategy for you. Unfortunately, for the rest of us, especially those of us who are introverted, walking up to strangers, picking a topic of conversation, finding an opening to jump in, and making sure it doesn't get awkward is terrifying. It's scary for a reason: in the early years of humanity, we were rarely, if ever, exposed to strangers. We would have been born into a small community and known everyone, or at least about them, since childhood.

The problem with networking is the same one most strategies for success come up against: unless we really train ourselves to develop a skill, it is nearly impossible to make it a habit, and even harder to enjoy it. Networking may work well for one out of one hundred, but the approaches we are looking for need to work regardless of your wealth, how introverted or shy you are, what country you are in, your race, or your gender, and they need to be enjoyable or you will never do them. This brings us to one of the most effective, fundamentally human, and enjoyable approaches for success that exist: being a part of a strong community.

If you were to connect with inspiring minds and respected leaders across the industries, and then consistently connect those people to each other, those relationships would foster a community in a short time. Just like the obesity study demonstrated, a community curated with people who have the characteristics you admire would benefit everyone involved. Not only would you develop skills and positive habits in the areas *you* care about most, but the other community members would benefit in the areas that matter to *them*. Everyone is better off. For Jean, not only did she lose weight, but so did the other women in the group. For you, the benefit might be career development, parenting, academics, or, like the abolitionists, a moral and ethical cause.

NETWORKING: IT CAN WORK FOR SOME, BUT MOST PEOPLE DON'T ENJOY IT

If you are like most people, when you hear the words "networking event," you get excited about the potential to make incredible contacts that can elevate your career, help you find your next job, and connect with new clients so you can meet sales goals. Just kidding . . . when most of us hear those two words we are filled with dread. Even though there are countless books, seminars, and events dedicated to making us better at it, the reality is that networking is incredibly uncomfortable, not that effective, and kind of awful for most of us.

WHY?

Dr. David Burkus, an organizational psychologist and author of the book *Friend of a Friend . . . : Understanding the Hidden Networks That Can Transform Your Life and Your Career*, has spent the past fifteen years examining the social structures of relationships. He explains it like this:

If you are at a networking event with one hundred people, chances are only a handful of them are going to be your ideal business contact. When the odds are four out of one hundred, you have to speak to twenty-five people on average in order to meet one potential contact, and that's assuming you two find a way to have a good conversation. People often refer to it as a "numbers game," but relating to people as numbers turns them into commodities. Now you have to cycle through people as quickly as possible so you can meet that one person you can do business with. It is an uncomfortable way to view humans, and it is also devoid of the characteristics that facilitate trust and connection. So you see these narcissistic networkers running through an event, passing you their card before they know your name, and leaving the conversation the moment they realize you don't have an immediate business value because it's a numbers game, and they have to hit their goal.

It's like the Hunger Games, but somehow less appealing and the odds are worse.

It is no surprise that Dr. Burkus has come to this conclusion: for most of us, networking is awful.

HOW BAD IS IT?

Francesca Gino and Tiziana Casciaro did a study comparing people's associations of networking for business purposes with making social connections or forming friendships. What they discovered is that people have an unconscious association of feeling dirty when they think about professional networking and are more likely to feel the need to clean themselves. This association didn't exist when they thought about connecting for friendship. They theorized that "such feelings of dirtiness decrease the frequency of [networking] and, as a result, work performance."[10]

Dr. Burkus believes that professional networking feels dirty because it lacks a sense of community. You've met most of your personal friends through your existing friends and activities, and you probably stayed friends because of a connection, not a transaction.[11] This is why researchers found that MBA students spend most of their time at networking events speaking to people they already know even though they feel obligated to make new contacts.

CONCLUSION

If you really optimize your networking, you may be able to get some phenomenal results, but it is unlikely to be as gratifying or fun as being part of a community with strong relationships.

As the person at the heart of your community, you wouldn't need industry awards or status. The value you would bring would be something wildly more unique: an invitation. After all, an invitation from you to meet and connect with your community members in a meaningful way would make you far more influential than any one award winner or thought leader. You would become a central figure in a community where everyone has an opportunity to succeed and, if done right, you would have the trust and access to move your career forward, popularize your ideas, market your products, grow your company, or whatever else is important to you. Invariably our potential grows with the success and strength of our community.

I wish I could say that when I started my goals were as lofty as changing the course of a nation or transforming the health of millions. I just wanted to bring people I admired together. For a broke twenty-eight-year-old, this was incredibly ambitious—after all, the people I was inviting were also being courted by global brands that were spending fortunes pampering them. I couldn't compete, so I didn't. Instead I realized I had to find a way to give them a unique experience, something they would never think of doing themselves. Since most of these guests could afford luxury, I gave them the opposite. I would give them the opportunity to come to my home, cook me dinner, wash my dishes, and clean my floors. The most amusing thing is, they thanked me for it.

It was not despite the effort they put in and the lack of luxury that this approach succeeded, but because of it. When an experience is designed well, not only will everyone be better off at the end, but it doesn't need to be expensive. My first dinner guests were people I knew, and no, I didn't know any Nobel laureates or celebrities. My parents are immigrants, and we just didn't know people like that. But as word of mouth spread, the guests became more impressive. In time, I learned how to refine the process of finding and inviting people and organizing the experience so that everyone felt included.

In the decade since its launch, I have hosted thousands of people at hundreds of dinners. As of publishing this book, the Influencers is active in ten cities and three countries and growing. Before the COVID-19 outbreak, every month we would host four or five dinners to bring in new members and five or more cultural events to bring the community back together to bond. As a result of the pandemic we started hosting digital events.

I got all the things that twenty-eight-year-old me was looking for. I worked out with Navy SEALs to get in shape, paid off all my debts, gave a TED Talk, traveled to all seven continents, was named one of the most eligible bachelors in America by *Elle*, was a science consultant for a popular TV show, launched a successful consultancy that helps companies connect with their customers and employees in meaningful ways, developed an international speaking career, and as of this writing, my first book is being turned into a TV show by a successful show runner, and the list goes on. But that isn't the important part. After a few years of running the dinners, we launched a nonprofit called Influence for Good, which brings important social issues to light and uses the support of the community to make an impact. We also started gatherings dedicated solely to women, people of color, and people who identify as LGBTQIA. We realized that as influence increases, so does the need to use it for a greater purpose.

Much like Jean, I never imagined that a well-placed invitation would lead to such a profound change in our lives. It just goes to prove that what fundamentally defines the quality of our lives is the people we are connected to, how much they trust us, and the sense of community we share.

The fact is, it doesn't matter if you are a parent tying to help your child in school, an introverted first-year associate trying to make a name for yourself, the chief revenue officer of a global company looking to attract customers and increase brand status, a nonprofit focused on funding and bringing awareness to an issue, or a civil rights activist starting a grassroots movement; this book's approach works. Why? Because it is about what it means to be human, what affects our decisions and our behavior, and, best of all, what creates deep and meaningful connections and gives us a sense of community. It's not about technology, AI, machine learning, or anything else you need a PhD to understand. All those things are wonderful, but they just can't replace the strength of exceptional communities and the trust between people. So, let's take a look at what we need to create these connections.

In the first part of this book, we will explore the Influence Equation. I will demonstrate the science of how we can connect with anyone, how to build trust quickly, and what creates a sense of community, so we can accomplish what we care about. These elements include:

Trust: Is trust a good thing? Do we even need it? We will learn the odd but true secrets of how trust works from one of the most famous medical doctors in British history. We will discover what sororities, U.S. Marines, and Swedish furniture have in common, and why it might be the best way to get people to care about you. We will explore the techniques used by the world's most successful cutlery salesman and what scientists call the "halo" effect. We will learn an essential and mostly unknown process to build trust, and then step into a lab to see how a single molecule causes it to work. By the end you will understand why we trust, how trust works, and how to win it quickly.

Connection: What causes people to connect? It won't surprise you that it depends on their degree of influence. After all, global leaders like Oprah and Sir Richard Branson have very different lives from industry leaders like CMOs of large companies and editors-in-chief of media outlets, and their lives are different from people who influence a community such as religious leaders or up-and-coming talent. We will explore the best approaches for each group and what it takes to engage them. We will speak with a real estate developer who sold his properties for more than two and a half times what his neighbors were charging during a recession, and while they went bankrupt, he became a huge success, thanks to his ability to connect. We will learn how the most absurd art heist in history caused the world to fall in love with a painting, and how this effect leads us to love our technology and food. We will take a quick trip to learn about a $50,000 event ticket that gives you the privilege of standing in the cold, surrounded by slush, and then visit Berlin to understand how a soft drink that tastes like medicine rose to popularity by opening a music school. Finally, you will learn why, if you are broke and don't know anyone, you might be in the ideal situation to connect with the people you admire most, and how to use all this knowledge to reach out to the people who matter most to you.

A Sense of Community: How do you create a tightly knit, highly supportive community from the people you connect with? To understand this, we will see what makes groups work from getting fit and fighting for social justice to building a great company culture, succeeding in business, and helping your friends. We begin with a visit with one of the most respected professional sports teams in the world, read about an obscure Wikipedia page that led to a massive internet argument, and learn how an unknown geeky kid living in his parents' home changed the comic book and entertainment industries. In the process we will discover the four things that give people a sense of community, how important they are to happiness, job satisfaction, health, and wealth, and how you can use them to improve the lives of all those around you.

In the second part of the book, we will combine the parts of the Influence Equation (connection, trust, and community) with a simple approach for applying it. We will explore fascinating discoveries in behavioral science and learn how to apply them to create opportunities to bring people together and for you to develop the relationships that are important to you. We will explore:

Biases and Mechanics: When you understand how people make decisions and perceive the world, you will probably laugh; we are completely ridiculous. We will explore how to predict human behavior by speaking to a criminal profiling expert and discover the behavioral quirks that we are all susceptible to, and how the top brands use them to drive our behavior. We will learn why there is a twenty-three-minute ferry ride from the ticket booth at Disney World to the front entrance (it's not for convenience), how companies like Apple price their products (you might get annoyed), and what percentage of our brains we really use—and what would happen if people used more.

The Path: Knowing people's mechanics is part of the answer; the other part is understanding the journey that we will design for them. From how they hear about our brand, cause, or product to when they have a sense of loyalty or membership, there are a lot of considerations along the way. To accomplish this, we learn the analogy of the elephant and the rider and look at how we can guide people on a journey they will love. By the end, we will develop a toolbox for understanding how to connect with people and design enjoyable and memorable experiences that bond them and help them understand you/your brand and each other better.

Part III is about you bringing your newfound knowledge of human behavior and the Influence Equation to life. We will bring together the people who are most important to you, in a way where everyone's life improves, and you will be at the center of it.

The Relationships That Matter to You: Whatever your goals are, by the end of this book you want to feel confident that you can develop relationships across any area of interest and a sense of community for all those you connect with. We will look at what it takes to apply these ideas across business relationships, company culture, social causes, and personal relationships, and examples of each so that you can find an approach that is right for your personality and interests regardless of how shy or introverted you are. It will excite you to grow and improve, and as you do, you will consistently get closer to your goals. We will look at ultra-low-cost experiences like games nights, luxury high-end experiences like secret brunches by a floral company and celebrity summer camps, and everything in between. The beauty is that communities often form best when resources are low, so regardless of who you are, we will find something that works for you so you can begin inviting.

So now I have an invitation for you (and you may have noticed my invitations are well worth accepting). This invitation is to discover how good life can get, to see what is really affecting our decisions, what makes us successful, and best of all to see who your next friend could be, because that next friend could affect your life in more ways than you can imagine. This is an invitation to discover the influence you can have in the areas you care about most. After all, once you understand how all of these ideas work together, and how they lead to success and influence, the only question will be what do you want to do with it? So, the choice is yours. Would you like to join me?

Chapter 2

The Benefit of Belonging

―――――

There was no way around it, according to a report by Congressmen Robert Steele and John Murphy:[1] the United States was about to face one of the biggest health crises in its two hundred–year history. Early estimates found that anywhere from 15 to 20 percent of enlisted troops in Vietnam had become addicted to heroin during their tour. That is as many as one in five soldiers, and they were returning home at a rate of about one thousand a day.

President Richard Nixon took swift action. One month later, on June 17, 1971, he held a press conference, declaring drug abuse "public enemy number one in the United States." To fight this enemy, he announced the creation of the Special Action Office for Drug Abuse Prevention (SAODAP), to be headed by Dr. Jerome Jaffe,[2] a leading methadone treatment specialist.

People were worried, and for good reason. As Dr. Jaffe explained: "The idea of 150 untreated heroin addicts trained in combat, coming in every day, was not one that made people feel comfortable."

Jaffe quickly met with a group of generals and colonels, and within two and a half weeks launched Operation Golden Flow, mandating that all servicemen subject themselves to urine testing before boarding planes back to the United States. (Yes, they actually called a urine testing program Operation Golden Flow, but what they lacked in subtlety they made up for in their speed and desire to help the troops.) To reduce the potential for incident, any person who tested positive would be held in Vietnam for treatment before returning home.

Unfortunately, anyone who has experienced addiction or seen its effects knows how hard it is to permanently kick the habit. The drug use relapse rates in the general population are incredibly high, estimated at 32 to 88 percent depending on how long individuals are tracked.[3] So, starting that September, researchers began tracking hundreds of veterans over the course of years to see how severe this problem was and how to tackle it.

As the data began to emerge, people braced for the worst. After all, we have always been taught "once an addict, always an addict." They expected horrible news. But what the data showed was far stranger than they could have predicted. Drug use had essentially dropped to the same standard levels as the general population. It made no sense. Heroin is extremely addictive; how could more than a hundred thousand people just stop, cold turkey?

To understand this phenomenon and what it has to do with our goal of creating meaningful connections with people who are important to us, we need to visit the strangest theme park in history: Rat Park. This playground was created in the 1970s by Canadian psychologist Bruce Alexander. You may be thinking *Disney has a park with a giant mouse, this might be something similar*, but Rat Park is not for humans. It's for rats.

Dr. Alexander was looking at drug addiction research in which rats were put in small boxes and given the option of drinking either plain water or water infused with morphine. Within a short time, the rats were consuming so much morphine water that they were dying. The research served as evidence that once people were hooked on drugs, they would continue to use until they died. But what if there was a different interpretation, Dr. Alexander thought. What if it wasn't the addictive quality of morphine alone, but also the profound isolation and boredom of being stuck in a small cage that caused the rats to become addicts? After all, in most prisons the worst punishment is solitary confinement. Many consider this kind of extended isolation inhuman, as it can trigger a wide range of mental health problems, from depression and hallucinations to schizophrenia and self-harm. Rats, much like humans, are social animals. If you were trapped alone in a small cage for weeks with nothing to do, chances are you would choose the morphine water too.

To test his theory, Dr. Alexander created Rat Park, an ideal playground where rats could socialize and play with their favorite toys. He made both plain water and morphine water available and then compared what they consumed to what was consumed by rats in isolated cages. The results were staggering, although, as Dr. Alexander says, "Some rats like to party."[4] Those in Rat Park barely drank the morphine water compared to those in isolation.

If drug abuse was purely about having access and exposure, then the rats of Rat Park would have all been addicts, just like the rats in isolation. It suggests that there must be another element beyond the drug itself that leads to addiction.

In response, Dr. Alexander developed the Dislocation Theory of Addiction, which explains that it is a lack of attachment, belonging, identity, meaning, and purpose that actually causes the opportunity for addiction. When someone is dislocated it "exacts a high price, because it ultimately generates misery in the form of anxiety, suicide, depression, disorientation, hopelessness, and resentful violence."[5] Consider for a moment a time when you were depressed or anxious, maybe even a time you felt hopeless or possibly considered suicide. If every day felt like this state of dislocation for us, it would only be a matter of time before we were willing to try anything not to feel this social pain. In a state of dislocation, drugs may seem like a great option.

Dislocation theory suggests that it isn't the drugs alone that make rats and people addicts, but the dislocation created by the confinement. It would explain why so many soldiers who were trapped in Vietnam, isolated from their friends and community, and feeling that they were fighting a war without meaning and purpose became addicts, but when they came back to their friends, family, and loved ones, they no longer had to fill that isolation with heroin. They once again felt whole.

Because we are a social species, dislocation is particularly painful. We will do anything to escape it, regardless of the consequences. After all, heroin users aren't naive to the dangers or health risks, and those who are susceptible to addiction come from every walk of life there is. This is an important point on human connection: from the outside it may seem that people's lives are perfect. But there is no lack of famous, successful, and beautiful people who suffer from dislocation and have become addicts, and it's not because they lack knowledge, shame, or empathy. But what they do have, if Dr. Alexander is right, is an incredible level of pain. In fact, research by Dr. Matt Lieberman, social psychologist and author of the book *Social: Why Our Brains Are Wired to Connect,* examined the significant impact of social pain (loss, rejection, alienation, loneliness, etc.) and how we process it through a simple group video game called Cyberball.

Imagine playing a simple ball-tossing video game with two other people. You have a ball and could pass it to either of your playmates. Once they catch it, they can throw it back to you or the other player. Initially you are all tossing to each other, and then something strange happens. They stop throwing it to you. Five, ten, fifteen throws, they ignore you completely with no end in sight. You have been excluded by the other players. How does it feel?

Lieberman put participants in an fMRI for a brain scan and had them play the game. He found that the areas of the brain that register the distress of physical pain were more active when participants were being left out of the game. In fact, the more someone said they felt bad about being left out, the stronger the activity was. As a culture, we tend to rank physical pain as more significant than social pain. If you were to hit someone, there could be significant legal punishment, but almost nothing like this exists for those who inflict social pain such as verbal abuse or bullying. Lieberman's research demonstrates that both social and physical pain are simply pain. This explains why, for many of us, the most painful moments of our lives involve social pain like losing a loved one. While a broken bone is painful at the time, once it heals properly, we tend not to recall the pain to the same degree as we remember and reexperience social pain. Thinking about an emotional trauma or loss can trigger anxiety, sadness, and depression among other responses.

In the next round of tests, Lieberman and his team took the experiment one step further. Participants were asked to take the painkiller Tylenol for two weeks before playing the game, but secretly half were taking a placebo. Then something fascinating happened. For those taking the real painkiller, the effects of social pain from exclusion disappeared. Just as physical pain is diminished by painkillers, so were the effects of social pain. Meanwhile, those who had taken the placebo felt just as much social pain from exclusion as the first group who took nothing.

If there was any doubt before, now it had been put to rest: regardless of the source, social or physical, pain is pain. For soldiers in Vietnam, doing drugs didn't just feel good, it also stopped them from feeling bad. Although only temporarily, it diminished the social pains of dislocation, and once they were home and those social pains likely disappeared, there was no reason to keep medicating.

The risk of social isolation and loneliness isn't limited to pain and drug addiction—it affects us at a much deeper level. Research has shown that those who are lonely are not only less focused, productive, and engaged, but they also die younger. It seems that if we want to be effective, taking some time to connect with friends and coworkers isn't a distraction so much as a productivity hack. From a health perspective, being lonely is on par with smoking almost a pack a day. The effect isn't just mental—a change happens at the cellular level. It puts us in a stressful state that has been shown to weaken our immune systems, reduce the quality of our sleep, and even strain our hearts, potentially leading to heart attack.[6]

We currently have an incredible opportunity to connect with people in a meaningful way. We are facing a loneliness epidemic, the kind we have never known as a species. A study conducted by health service provider Cigna found that nearly half of Americans report sometimes or always feeling alone (46 percent) or left out (47 percent). In fact, the younger a person was, the more likely they were to express loneliness. The groups most affected by loneliness are Gen Z (those just entering the workforce) and millennials. These hyper-connected, internet-using, texting, social media–posting generations may be more digitally connected than any before, but they are also more isolated. The fact is that digital relationships don't make up for person-to-person contact. A separate study found that 22 percent of millennials in the United States say they have *no* friends, and 30 percent say they always or often feel lonely. That is a rate twice or more than baby boomers (born 1944–1964)—9 percent say they have no friends and 15 percent are always or often lonely.[7]

It may be tempting to think that we simply get less lonely with age, but isolation is a social trend. Over the course of two decades from the mid-1980s to mid-2000s, the average American went from having almost 3 close friends (2.94) to just over 2 (2.08).[8] Considering the significant impact and social pain of loneliness, this has a profound and dire health impact on our society. This is also why taking an approach built around human relatedness is so important—people are truly in need of it. Connecting, building trust, and being a part of a community aren't just about increasing your success or health, or pushing a social cause; they are about improving everyone's life in the process.

The situation may sound dire, but there is a silver lining. Dr. Lieberman points out that if we feel the impact of social cues so deeply, they must be incredibly useful and might even be our superpower. Those same characteristics that make us need social interaction also allow us to relate to one another and associate more effectively. What allowed us to survive as a species was not incredible speed, superior physical strength, or an ability to go long distances without food or water. Those advantages all belong to other species. In fact, compared to much of the animal kingdom, we are frail and weak and should have died out a long time ago, except for one thing: we can work together. We can coordinate to hunt down large animals and build shelters that protect us from the elements. We can relate to and understand each other beyond language. A newborn doesn't need to speak for their mother to understand her; her mother can empathize.

Lieberman believes that we need to reexamine Maslow's hierarchy of needs. At the bottom currently are physical needs like food, water, and shelter, then up a level are the psychological needs like friendship and a sense of relatedness, and at the top is self-actualization, you being the best you. Lieberman would suggest that the psychological elements may also belong at the bottom as the most essential. A newborn wouldn't survive long if their mother couldn't relate to their needs. What has let us survive as a species is our ability to form relationships. It is these characteristics that give us our greatest opportunity to empathize and develop relationships with the people who can have the biggest effect on the areas of life we care about the most.

Nowhere does this become clearer than in the middle of the Mediterranean, on a small island near Sardinia, Italy, in a village made of tightly packed interwoven buildings and homes. If you were to peek inside one of these homes on a Sunday, there is a good chance you would see a grandmother with her daughter and granddaughter preparing the local specialty known as culurgiones. They are like large ravioli pockets filled with high-fat ricotta and mint that are served with delicious tomato sauce. As they work away in the small kitchen and dining area, they share stories and gossip and enjoy the occasional stop-in by a neighbor or relative.

What you would never guess is that village holds a secret, not only what Dan Buettner calls a blue zone, one of the few places in the world where people live much longer than the average (there are six times more centenarians than on the Italian mainland just two hundred miles away and ten times more than in the United States), but according to Dr. Susan Pinker, psychologist and author of *The Village Effect: How Face-to-Face Contact Can Make Us Healthier and Happier*, it is the only place in the world where men and women live to the same age.[9] Elsewhere, throughout the world, women on average live six to eight years longer than men.

Dr. Pinker jokes about the culurgiones in her TED Talk: clearly "a low-fat, gluten-free diet is not what it takes to live to one hundred in the blue zone."[10] So, what is?

This is the question that challenged Dr. Julianne Holt-Lunstad, whose research at Brigham Young University looked at tens of thousands of people and examined everything from diet and smoking habits to marital status and exercise to try to understand what leads to longevity. After seven years of tracking their group, they had an answer, and it wasn't what anyone expected.

Although clean air has a small positive impact on life expectancy, it wasn't nearly as important as having a flu vaccine and exercising, and those weren't as important as quitting drinking and smoking. What surprised the researchers the most, and should be obvious to you by now, was that the greatest predictors by far were relationships. Close relationships had the second greatest impact. Those people we can rely on when we are in trouble, those with whom we can talk through a problem we are having, who can lend us money when we are in a pinch, or who can pick up our kids if we have to work late. It makes sense that these emotional connections would be essential, but what was completely unexpected was that the most important predictor of living a long life was what researchers call social integration.[11] This is how many people you talk to or connect with throughout the day. It could be your dry cleaner, a colleague at work, or the person at your yoga class. These connections aren't necessarily close friends, but rather people you engage with. Dr. Holt-Lunstad's research suggests that if you want to live a long and enjoyable life, the most important thing you can do is surround yourself with people and develop both deep, meaningful relationships and loose associations. The best thing for us might be to cancel our Amazon Prime and actually go to the local store, meet the person at the register, and buy the things we need. The time we save on two-day delivery might just be reducing our life span.

Without connection we suffer a slew of negative effects on our health, productivity, and satisfaction, and we are currently seeing unprecedented levels of loneliness and disconnection.

Now let's get to the good news for all of us: every problem we described, from longevity and focus, to productivity and dislocation, is solved or seriously diminished by having close relationships and loose associations.

Human connection is something we are all capable of, regardless of how shy we are. Even if it may feel uncomfortable at times, we all have this capability, otherwise we would not have survived as a species. This means each of us has an incredible potential to connect. It doesn't require a lot of money or special skills to solve this problem; we can improve the quality of our lives and the lives of others at almost no expense.

Which brings us to you. In the first chapter you saw that bringing people together, being at the center of a community, can have a profound impact on the things you care about. But creating community isn't just something you are doing for yourself. People need connection now more than ever. This may sound cliché, but the research supports it. Chances are high that the people you want to connect with are in need of connection too and may not even realize it. Being successful, famous, wealthy, or important doesn't make you immune from being human or needing to create meaningful relationships. What we gain in modern society from convenience may in fact isolate us. Whereas if we were born on a small island in the Mediterranean, we would feel profoundly connected. So, now we will explore what allows us to connect with those who are most important to us, and in the process create a better life for everyone involved.

Trust

Chapter 3

What Trust Is Made Of

———

After graduating medical school in 1970, Dr. Harold Frederick Shipman worked as a physician at hospitals and in private practices. In 1993, he opened his own private practice in the town of Hyde, not far from Manchester, England, and grew it to more than three thousand patients, many of them elderly. Fred, as people called him, wasn't a legendary surgeon, or known for publishing brilliant papers in academic journals, but he was well liked and trusted in the community. He was known to many as the "good" doctor. He had gentle eyes, a nonthreatening demeanor, and a lovely wife and four children, and as his beard whitened with age he looked more and more like Santa.

In the summer of 1998, Angela Woodruff was grieving her mother, Kathryn's, passing. One morning, a few days after her death, an unexpected letter arrived in the mail, stating that her mother had updated her will just days before her death. The inheritor of her mother's assets was now Dr. Shipman, her mother's physician. Angela was confused. Was it possible that in her elder years, her mother had become so close to the Shipman family that they replaced her own daughter? Could she have owed the doctor money in some way?

This wasn't the first time something strange happened around Dr. Shipman. A few months earlier the local coroner had noticed an unusual number of patients whose death certificates were signed by the good doctor. It may not be uncommon for a caring physician who does house visits and is close with his elderly patients, the coroner reasoned. Dr. Shipman may simply be the first call the family makes when their loved one passes. But something felt strange. Even though there was likely nothing to be concerned about, as a precaution the coroner informed the authorities, and an investigation was launched.

Angela, being a solicitor in England, what Americans would call a non-courtroom lawyer, decided to track down the witnesses to her mother's will. But when Angela finally found one of the witnesses, what she discovered shocked her. While performing a procedure on Kathryn, Dr. Shipman called in patients from the waiting area to sign what they thought was a consent form, confirming and witnessing that Kathryn was agreeing to a medical procedure. Although the paper was folded over and only showed the signature lines, there was no reason for them to doubt it was anything other than a standard medical form. So, they signed and then returned to the waiting room, thinking nothing of it and not knowing that they had signed both Kathryn's will and her death sentence. A few days later, Dr. Shipman came to Kathryn's home and pronounced her dead.

When Angela contacted investigators, she could never have predicted the true depths of what Dr. Shipman had done. Between Angela's complaint and the suspicions from the coroner, police exhumed fifteen bodies to search for evidence. By the time their investigation was completed, it became clear that the "good" doctor Fred was Dr. Death, England's most prolific serial killer.

Over the course of twenty-three years (1975–1998) under the cover of a caring and compassionate physician, Dr. Shipman had murdered anywhere from 215 to 265 or more people, making him one of the most lethal serial killers in history. Many of his victims were given a lethal dose of morphine in a fashion similar to the way Shipman's mother would receive her cancer pain medication.

It boggles the mind. Shipman was married, had kids and thousands of patients, and no one noticed the atrocities he was committing. The strangest part was that his undoing was not murder, but fraud. How is that even possible? How could so many people die over almost a quarter century before someone doubted him? And what does this mean for us as we look to develop deep and meaningful relationships with people?

Trust, you could say, is willingness to be vulnerable. The more you trust someone, the more vulnerable you are willing to be with them. It's important to note that it is often based on a specialty. Chances are you don't trust your plumber to do your taxes, or your best friend to perform your heart surgery, but you would tell your best friend your secrets, fears, or maybe what embarrasses you. This is because being vulnerable with your health or finances is safest when professionals have specialized knowledge and experience. We all know that being vulnerable with someone who has bad intentions can have dire results, from heartbreak and theft to the loss of life. So, we need to first understand why people trust. Then we can determine if someone deserves ours and demonstrate that we are worthy of theirs.

Dr. Kent Grayson runs the Trust Project at the Kellogg School of Management. He and his colleagues from across the sciences and philosophies come together to explore the latest research and ideas about how trust works, when it fails us, and what to do when we need to repair it. For the most part, researchers like Grayson agree that trust is made up of three basic pillars:

1. *Competence:* The ability to do something successfully. Hopefully you would be concerned if you found out your neurosurgeon was a five-year-old. That's not ageism; someone that young just couldn't have the competence necessary to perform the delicate work it takes surgeons years to develop. On the other hand, you should feel confident that if a chef has earned a Michelin star, they are capable and proficient with the skills necessary to make you some lunch.

2. *Honesty/Integrity:* The person or company is truthful, their product will do what they say it will do, they are not misleading

us, and if they do find an issue, they will acknowledge and correct it.

3. *Benevolence:* They are acting with your best interests in mind. When you take your car in for repairs, you want to know that the mechanic is doing the repairs you need, not anything extra in order to get paid more or hit quota.

According to Grayson, there are several factors that can affect the depth of that trust, and we will explore those, but these three provide the foundation. Even among them, some are more fragile and some lean more heavily on the others. For example, if someone you consider competent messes up, you probably will brush it off as a singular incident or bad day. If your hairstylist forgets to put your appointment in the calendar, you wouldn't label them incompetent, or if Google Maps or Waze confuses an address for another area, you would likely continue to use the service. But if a person or brand were to demonstrate weakness in the other pillars, like a lack of honesty (they lied to you) or a lack of benevolence (they were exclusively self-interested), you would lose trust in them right away. These pillars will define whether someone will want to do business with you or donate to your cause, how well your employees interact, and how much influence you develop. In light of this, we need to understand how they function.

If you caught someone in a significant lie, wouldn't you begin to doubt everything they say? In the long term, this breach could be repaired, but for now you would likely question anything they say. We tend not to take deception lightly, but there is an exception—if the dishonesty was for a benevolent reason. Imagine you are barhopping with some friends, and just as you all are about to enter a lounge, one of your friends pokes their head in, and then says to skip it because this place looks boring. You move on, and later that night you find out that your recent ex was there on a date. Would you be mad at your friend for lying? Probably not—you would understand that they were trying to protect you from needless pain. If on the other hand the lie was to cover up that your ex was on a date with someone you know, you may not consider the dishonesty to be benevolent and you may lose trust in your friend.

Grayson points out that people judge a breach of benevolence over that of honesty and judge a breach of honesty more harshly than a breach of competence. You may have noticed that companies that breach consumer trust tend to blame the issue as a temporary slip-up in competence. If your bank pulled money from your account that they shouldn't have, they don't want you thinking it was a breach of honesty or benevolence, since those are much tougher to repair. Instead, they'll explain that it was a programing issue, and that they have not only corrected the mistake but created a team to make sure it doesn't happen again. With an excuse of competence, whether it is true or not, most people will be forgiving and move on. If we take away anything from Grayson's research, it should be how important it is for us to always lead with benevolence. When people know that we have their best interests at heart and that we have a reputation for honesty, the competence part can be improved over time.

Now we begin to see why it took so long for the people of Hyde to notice Dr. Death's activities. For starters, according to a large national survey, medical professionals (nurses and medical doctors) are considered the most trustworthy people in our culture. You expect them to be competent in their work (there is stringent training and testing), honest (there are ethical and medical reviews, required documentation and procedures, and strict laws), and benevolent (we view medicine as a profession for those who care about others).

So, when Dr. Shipman's patients passed away, it wasn't seen as a lack of competence or that he was negligent; instead it would have been brushed off as an old patient whose time had come. After all, not everyone can be healed. As a doctor, a patient's death is a loss of a customer, so there would be no reason for anyone to think he was dishonest or lacked benevolence. As a result, Dr. Death was able to kill more than two hundred people. His downfall was not a breach of competence but a breach of honesty and benevolence. It wasn't as easy to brush off the suspicion of forging papers to gain the inheritance of a vulnerable eighty-two-year-old woman.

People often say we need more trust in the world. But clearly a lack of trust wasn't the issue with Dr. Shipman. In the years since, the British medical system has placed additional oversight on the profession to ensure nothing like that happens again. But given the devastating impact wrongly placed trust can have (heartbreak, theft, death, etc.), it raises the question: Why, as a species, do we trust others at all?

Imagine it's forty thousand years ago, and a pregnant mother gives birth to a daughter. She is exhausted after labor, and the newborn wants to feed. Fortunately, the mother has stored up some supplies, but the stress of childbirth and caring for her daughter are significant. Within a few days the food will run out. Even if she had enough energy and strength to climb a tree and gather fruits/vegetables/nuts, how will she do it while carrying and protecting a child? If the child cries, it might alert animals hunting for their next meal. How will she and the baby survive?

They probably wouldn't. When taking into account the faster metabolism our species used to have, the availability of food, and the physical limitations of the human body, we see that we are just not designed to go through life alone. While a deer can give birth to a baby fawn and both are able to run minutes later, human children don't possess independence until years after birth. A single mother with a baby probably wouldn't have been able to survive long without some kind of community support.

Unfortunately, this is where the survival paradox kicks in. If engaging with people means we can be hurt and taken advantage of, then it makes sense to be defensive all the time, but if not engaging means we don't get the support we need to survive, then we are stuck. We are damned if we do and damned if we don't. So, we need a system to decide when that risk is worth it and when it's not. This is why trust exists. Even though there is a risk of being hurt, that risk doesn't come close to the risk of dying out as a species. We survive because we developed trust. As a by-product, we created functional communities in which members hunted and gathered in groups, where children could play with one another, and where people could come together to protect one another from outside threats. It also meant people developed specialties like medicine, construction, and cooking, and as a species we could become more effective. This isn't a perfect system—it means that at times people are deceived or robbed, tribalism grows, or extreme cases like Dr. Shipman emerge—but the occasional anomaly is much better than inevitable extinction.

You will notice that whether you trust someone or not seems to flow naturally. Because of accepted cultural norms, I have an institutional trust in New York City's public transportation system, so I don't think my bus driver is going to try to steal my money. In cultures where institutional trust is lower, people may be constantly concerned about being scammed. Regardless of which situation you are in, you will notice that you don't evaluate each person or company from scratch. Not only would it take a long time and may involve references, credit checks, and an interview, but this would be a lot of work just to get a hamburger at a supermarket. To accomplish that level of consideration, our brains would constantly be on high alert, and we probably wouldn't have the focus to manage all the other things we need to do in a day. So, as we evolved, we developed shortcuts or biases that very quickly let us know if we should trust or not.

Consider for a moment how a hummingbird floats—its flapping wings look like a blur that defies the laws of physics. In the same amount of time it takes for a single flap, just 3/100th of a second,[1] the human brain can see a person and make an essential decision whether they can trust them. In the time it takes to show a single frame of a movie, people judge how worthy we are of their trust.

If influence is a by-product of connection, trust, and sense of community, this news is not encouraging. I would want someone to trust me because of my track record and reputation of integrity. Unfortunately, it seems that many of the factors that initially trigger trust are beyond our control, especially in the short term. How pronounced your cheekbones are,[2] the color of your eyes,[3] even the depth of your voice[4] will affect how trustworthy people think you are. You won't be surprised that none of these things have anything to do with a person's actual trustworthiness.

The problem we face is that initial impressions of trust are based on something we are preprogrammed with or learn from our culture; our snap judgments and biases happen almost instantaneously. Research suggests that if you see someone dressed like a nurse, you are far more likely to trust them than a car salesman or lobbyist.

Since none of us are going to get cheek implants, walk around in medical scrubs, and lower our voice just to be trusted more, what do we do?

First off, since we are looking to develop relationships in which everyone is better off, the context needs to be benevolent. I have to repeat this because in the business world objectives are often purely self-serving. Relationships are made to extract as much value as possible. Instead of creating deep and meaningful interactions, people are like vampires trying to get all they can. We can be fooled by these takers in the short run, but eventually their reputation catches up with them. This is equally true with honesty—it is very hard to recover from being found out as deceitful. But if you have a reputation for benevolence and honesty, competence becomes much easier to demonstrate, and then you have trust. But this still leaves one big problem: how to demonstrate our trustworthiness when we are constrained by time and at the mercy of the biases of the people we meet. One possible approach is to understand the mechanics of these biases and break down how they work. Then we can appeal to them and develop a base level of trust. Instead of being at the mercy of these decision-making shortcuts, we can use them to demonstrate our character to anyone who is important to us.

Chapter 4

The Science of Building Trust Quickly, aka Why Everyone Loves a Dombås

It is 9:45 p.m. and Steven Wilson's* workday is almost over. He is tired, his voice is sore, and his only desire in life is to get to his bed and sleep for a few hours, because tomorrow he has to wake up before sunrise and do it all again. Tonight he has earned his sleep. He can be proud of his work because he knows every single person who reports to him hates him. That's not normally something a well-adjusted person takes pride in, but for Steve it's a mark of success. In almost any other job, if your manager were to treat you the way Steve treats his reports, he or she would be fired. Clearly, he would prefer to be liked, but people's lives are on the line, and so he has a choice—be effective and hated or be liked and risk people dying.

Steve's reports aren't a standard office team. They aren't part of the marketing department or a division trying to develop an app. Steve is in charge of seventy new recruits, or "boots." His full name is Drill Instructor Staff Sergeant Steven Joseph Wilson United States Marine Corps. He, along with his fellow drill instructors, leads a group of new recruits at Marine Corps Recruit Depot Parris Island to prepare them for a life of service and, possibly, war. I don't share this story about a drill instructor because he is now a celebrity or billionaire. I

---

* Steven Joseph Wilson is a composite of several people I learned about while researching this book and is not a specific person.

share it because drill instructors are unsung heroes. They are ordinary people who produce results that should be impossible. In a matter of weeks, they take a group of people who have never met and get them to a level of care and trust so high that they would risk their lives for one another.

Let's be honest, most of us wouldn't trust a stranger with our wallets or our cell phones, but Steve will get a group of strangers from different religions, political views, races, and parts of the country, people who have nothing in common besides the coincidence of showing up to training on the same day, to become profoundly connected. And he only has a few weeks to do it. To understand how he accomplishes this, it's not enough to understand the pillars we discussed in Chapter 3; we also need to understand how those pillars are created. Since your relationships will only be as strong as the trust you share, I want you to become an expert at developing a deep sense of trust quickly.

You have probably noticed that the longer you know people, the more you tend to trust them. This is also true for companies and brands. Morning Consult is a research company that specializes in understanding what Americans think. They survey over ten million people a year and have a keen grasp of what we like and trust the most. When ranking the one hundred most trusted companies in America, their team discovered that only two of them were founded in the last twenty years; the other ninety-eight were far older, and many were over one hundred years old.[1] But as nice as it is to develop ever deepening relationships over the course of thirty or more years, neither Steve nor we have the luxury of that kind of time. We will often only have a few minutes or hours with someone. So, what are the other options?

Imagine you are at the entrance to your child's school and one of the parents you are friends with walks up to you. Before you can thank her for hosting your child at a playdate, she gently puts her hand on your shoulder and asks you to wish your mother a happy birthday. You are surprised and caught off guard. How did she remember? Did you mention it on the phone when you were planning the playdate? In that moment something wonderful happened—you began to trust her more.

People often think trust develops from grandiose actions like saving someone's life, throwing a surprise party, or giving a large gift, but research has shown that it is more a by-product of micro actions that demonstrate care and belonging. Things like asking about their children by name, remembering a birthday, or well-placed insightful compliments. These cues of being cared for and belonging to a community, group, or even friendship are incredibly impactful, especially over time. Granted, if you were to call up a client and recite a stalkerish level of knowledge about the person's family, it would probably freak them out. As long as it is within the bounds of normal behavior, demonstrating that you consistently remember, care, and show appropriate levels of physical contact (a pat on the shoulder, handshake, etc.) goes a long way. I have a family friend, Dana Goldberg, whose children I grew up with, and every year on August 19 at about 10 a.m. I get a call from her wishing me a happy birthday. I don't know how she remembers, and I'm positive it isn't a calendar reminder. The fact is, it feels special that she goes out of her way for me. It is no surprise we consider the Goldbergs trusted family friends. Once you know someone, take note of what is important to them and bring it up when you see each other or chat. You will notice how much it means to them that you remember and how much it strengthens your relationship.

Although these micro expressions of belonging can build up over time, neither Steve nor we can wait for them to create the significant levels of trust we want. So, we have to find an alternate approach. The answer we are looking for may be found in part by following the career of an older Italian man named Gino Leocadi.

When Gino's colleagues describe him, the word most often used is "legend," possibly because this seventy-nine-year-old man's peers are mostly college students, and that's the way college students describe people they respect. Gino has spent the past fifty-six years doing a job that, by most people's standards, sounds completely insane. He walks up to the homes of complete strangers, often women who are alone, with a bag full of knives and convinces them to open their doors and sit together so that he can sell them cutlery. Over the course of his career, he has sold over $5 million in kitchen products, an astounding amount when you consider that when he started a set of knives that now cost $3000 were only $169, and he did this all through one-on-one in-home presentations.

You may imagine Gino, a kindly, reserved man, as one of those classic door-to-door encyclopedia or vacuum cleaner salesmen types. But what Gino does is wildly more brilliant. He uses a behavioral shortcut called the "halo effect."

When these kitchen products were being sold door-to-door in the 1970s, it was grueling work full of the consistent rejection of having doors slammed in your face and people complaining that you were bothering them. But then a few salespeople asked a question: What if we could make sure new customers didn't see us as complete strangers? Could we get our existing customers to recommend us to their friends? Then we wouldn't have to build trust from scratch for every meeting; we would be building off a trusted relationship between friends.

The approach they developed was so successful that they formed Vector Marketing, the now exclusive provider of Cutco Cutlery. Most people know Cutco because a charmingly awkward college student came to their home and did a demonstration involving cutting a shiny penny with a pair of kitchen scissors and some rope and leather with a knife. I know this because I was one of those charmingly awkward college students; it's how I paid for college. In fact, Cutco/Vector hires about forty thousand recruits a year, many of them students for part-time work through their local offices, and each presentation they do is by direct referral. This means that aside from the initial practice that new independent sales representatives do with a few friends and family, every person who has seen and bought Cutco has done so because of an unbroken and ever-growing network of trust.

What makes this incredible is just how well this approach has worked. For the past thirty years Cutco has been the number one selling kitchen cutlery brand in America, and the only way anyone ever sees it is through direct referral. You can't find it in stores, and you have never seen a single ad for it, but year after year they outsell the top brands at Macy's, Williams Sonoma, and even Amazon.

Part of Cutco's incredible success is that it makes a phenomenal product, but what truly separates it from other brands is that its sales representatives leverage the halo effect. It works like this: if someone we trust is connected to a person, product, or service, we are more likely to trust those things. The effect is named after the mythical discs of light that emanate from holy people or angels, illuminating everything around them. Anything the light touches is brightened by the halo in the same way that anything touched by a person or brand we trust becomes more trusted.

This is the reason brands seek endorsements from popular personalities—not just because nowadays they have their own audiences on social media, but because of the boost in brand reputation. Whether or not Nike's Jordan brand sneakers and clothing are more attractive, better for athletes, or even connected in any meaningful way to Michael Jordan is questionable, but what isn't questionable is that in a single twelve-month period, Nike generated 3.14 billion dollars from the Jordan brand alone.[2] Similarly, an endorsement from a Kardashian or Jenner can sell out a dress in minutes. You might think you are somehow immune to this kind of behavioral bias, but if you ever tried a new flavor from a snack or drink brand you like, or met with someone, went to a movie, or ate at a restaurant on a friend's recommendation, you have experienced the halo effect. Let's be real—just because someone we trust recommends something doesn't guarantee it's good. Dr. Shipman's patients likely recommended him to people, and that may have ended terribly, but in most cases the halo effect provides a great shortcut to thinking. If I trust A, and A trusts B, then there is a good chance I will trust B. The fact is, we don't think about it—it is automatic.

What Gino does, possibly better than anyone else, is understand how to get himself into a halo of trust, simply because he was just in your friend's kitchen chatting with her. He understands that the more halos he can be associated with, the more trusted he is. Instead of just saying, "Susie said I should give you a call," he throws in a collection of other cues. He may emphasize that they were sitting together, having coffee, talking about her grandchildren, and if he was attentive that day, he may mention them by name. Since Susie was also recommended by someone, he may mention that they were originally connected through Jeannette, or her sister Maggie. He touches halo after halo, and eventually our brains will say he must be trustworthy. Within a two-minute conversation, Gino goes from being a random stranger to a member of the community who likely knows many of her friends. Gino has done such a great job of this that he has served generation after generation of the same families and communities, and in the process, he has developed lifelong relationships. For Gino it "feels like [he] is servicing his family."

Going from friend to friend, Gino and his colleagues have been able to sit with celebrities, billionaires, C-level executives at Fortune 500 companies, famous authors, and entrepreneurs. The beauty is that by leaning on the halo effect, they all have found a shortcut to trust that most of us never think of. Sure, we'll ask a friend for an occasional contact or introduction, but how many of us have continued the process so we can get an introduction to the people we admire most? Chances are, we have been underutilizing the halo effect, especially considering a 2016 Facebook study found that we are on average about 3.6 degrees of separation from anyone in the world, and probably far less for people in our culture.[3] That means that all it takes is a few good introductions and you could connect with anyone you want. If Gino has shown us anything, we can probably be building trust much faster. Unfortunately for Staff Sergeant Steven Wilson, the halo effect isn't strong enough to bond his recruits. For the halo effect to work, you need an initial point of trust that you can build from. For the recruits, it will kick in once they see themselves as

Marines. At that point, if they meet other Marines for the first time, the halo effect probably will create a sense of community and trust. But it still leaves the question: How do you trigger that initial development of trust? When I searched for this answer, I wasn't expecting to find it at a sorority.

Getting into a coveted college sorority can be a competitive, grueling experience. In many cases what separates those who get in from those who wash out is simply who can handle the pressure. When we think of sorority pledging, we tend to imagine binge drinking, body shaming, or even the sharing of secrets, but the rituals can vary dramatically and be much worse. In one sorority, the girls are told to face a concrete wall, and if they move slightly, even wiggle their arms or legs, their faces are knocked into the wall. In another, to prove their resolve, they are forced to hold burning hot coals[4] until they are given permission to release them. In others, they must stand in freezing cold water as they recite phrases from memory or are locked in a basement for hours while people come down periodically to interrogate them, hoping that they break and divulge secrets. In an incident a few years back, pledges were ordered to perform hours of beach and water calisthenics in the sweltering sun. Even though they were tired and worn out, they were ordered to enter the ocean backwards as wave after wave hit them. Two girls were pulled out to sea, overwhelmed by the heavy waves, and drowned.

When I share these examples, they probably sound less like sorority hazing and more like Steve's Marine Corps boot camp, elite special ops training for the U.S. Navy SEALs, or even the Russian military's Spetsnaz, but none of these groups would ever do these things, because their training, for the most part, is developed with a specific outcome in mind that makes sense.

For many sororities the pledging process enters the realm most people would consider malicious abuse. Oddly, though, for those who make it through the often sleepless weeks of hazing, something interesting happens on the other side. In the words of one sorority sister, "Even though that experience was awful, pledging was the most fun that I never want to have again, and as brainwashing as it sounds, it made me really genuinely care about my sorority and the girls in it."

Once someone goes through such an intense experience, it isn't surprising that they possess a profound comradery. These are clearly extreme examples involving both physical and psychological torment, but many cultures have their rites of passage to separate those who are accepted as part of the in-group or allow community members to earn their status of manhood or womanhood. On the milder side, Jewish children often read a portion of the Hebrew bible in front of their community. Comparatively, the Sateré-Mawé tribe of the Amazon have possibly one of the most painful traditions in the world. Young men line up for an opportunity to put on gloves that have been weaved with bullet ants so their stingers face in. Once the gloves are on, the ants continuously sting the person's hands, injecting what is considered the most painful toxin in the world. A single sting is thirty times more painful than a wasp's, and they are being stung hundreds of times.[5] While wearing the gloves, the young men dance in hopes of distracting themselves from the pain. Although the gloves come off after about five minutes, the ordeal lasts for about twenty-four hours as wave after wave of pain runs through them.[6] Alternatively, when the women of the Mentawai Islands reach puberty, they must beautify themselves by using a rock and chisel to file their teeth down to sharp points.[7] In Brazil, the Matis hunting trials involve the boys having poison put in their eyes, being beaten and whipped,[8] and then, using wooden needles, they inject themselves with the poison of the giant leaf frog.[9]

As you read this, you may realize two things. The first is that Westerners have it way easy. Our biggest concern is getting our driver's license, and soon cars will drive themselves. The other is that in every case, the participants put in an extraordinary amount of effort. You would expect that the effort would detract from the experience, but you would be wrong. It is not despite the effort that the sorority members value their sisters but because of it. As a by-product of going through the experience together and being in a vulnerable state, they begin to care for and trust one another. This is the missing piece of the solution to Steve's problem. The same mechanics that affect sorority girls pledging, the Sateré-Mawé tribe's men, and the women of the Mentawai Islands serve to bond Steve's recruits and have them put their lives in each other's hands. If you can understand why this works, you can develop the same level of trust that normally takes weeks or years in a few minutes or hours. To explain how this works, we turn to a Swedish furniture company that might be the world's expert on the topic.

If you have ever moved into a home, you likely have experienced your own rite of passage. Maybe you borrow the largest car you can get and drive to a massive store in hopes of finding everything you need. When you enter you realize the store is set up like a winding maze—there is no escape. Luckily, even though you can't pronounce the names of the products—Poäng, Dombås, Äpplarö—you can still buy them. After hours of collecting giant boxes containing tables, beds, chairs, and more, and at least one or two arguments with the person you are with, you then have to stand in line, pay, transport everything home, and begin the arduous task of assembling everything. If this sounds familiar, you have had the privilege of shopping at IKEA. What none of us realizes is that because we put so much effort into this experience, we disproportionately value our IKEA furniture. Mind you, you may not like it, but you value it far more than if it arrived fully formed in your home. This is what scientists call the IKEA effect, a well-documented human bias that causes us to care about the things we put effort into. For example, if on their eighteenth birthday you found out your child was switched at birth, you wouldn't stop loving the child you raised, and that's because you raised them. It is because of the sleepless nights, the cooking, the hours of homework, the colds, and all the things you will never remember you did that you love them. This is the IKEA effect in full force, and we are all at its mercy.

Between people this is sometimes referred to as the Ben Franklin effect. In his autobiography Franklin shares advice his father gave him. To paraphrase: someone who has done you a favor is more likely to do you another favor than someone who has never done you a favor. This advice became particularly useful when Ben needed to win over a contentious political rival. Instead of being nice to the man, Franklin asked to borrow a rare book from the man's library. Two hundred years ago, you couldn't just download an audible version, so the man had to go out of his way to bring it to Franklin, and after that they were friends until the man's passing.

The IKEA effect is the answer to our problem of how to build trust quickly with the people who can have the biggest impact on our lives, and the solution to the problem Steven has with his Marine boot camp. The fastest way to build trust between people who have nothing in common is to have them put collaborative effort into a common goal or problem, a kind of joint IKEA effect. But Steve isn't going to send them to buy and assemble furniture, so he needs another rallying point. Unfortunately for Steve, the only problem that his reports have in common is him. So, he does what any good drill instructor does—he makes sure they hate him more than anything they have ever known. They have a common problem; they hate Steve and don't want to get in trouble. This is a problem so big no one can tackle it on their own. Instead it becomes a rallying point. With each additional time Steve yells at them, disciplines them, or gives them an impossible task, they learn that the only way to survive boot camp is to work together.

With stakes being so high, they are highly motivated to solve the problem. Day and night, they put in effort supporting one another and making sure the group succeeds. As they do, they grow to care more about one another and unify so they can be above reproach. Over the course of boot camp, the comradery and bonding that connects the team then has a halo effect on the Marines in general. That effort bonds them and creates trust, and then the halo effect has the potential to spread that trust to the organization as a whole.

Having a drill instructor may work well for the military, but this isn't exactly a realistic approach to bond with a potential client you want to meet, a donor you want to support your cause, a new friend, or the employees of your company. But maybe an understanding of why this works can be used to impact our relationships and create the trust we need with anyone we want.

The process begins with finding a challenge big enough to require people to work together. If it's easy enough to do alone, there is no need to engage with others. The challenge can be as simple as stuffing envelopes to get wedding invitations out or serving food at a homeless shelter, or as complex as building a house for Habitat for Humanity or trying to launch a company. As you work together, there inevitably are moments when people need support. It may be physical (e.g., moving something too heavy to move alone), emotional (e.g., being overwhelmed and needing to decompress or vent), or intellectual (e.g., needing a new perspective or someone to help them solve a problem). In these moments, something wonderful happens between people that researcher Jeffrey Polzer refers to as a vulnerability loop.

Although people tend to believe that trust precedes vulnerability, Polzer and his team theorized the opposite to be true. Their work has shown that trust comes second through a very predictable process:

- Person 1: Signals vulnerability (says or does something that demonstrates a need from others)
- Person 2: Acknowledges the signal
- Person 2: Puts out a signal in return
- Person 1: Acknowledges Person 2's signal

Trust is increased between these two, creating an opportunity for another loop.

For example, if I say to you: "I have never done a project like this before—I'm totally overwhelmed," you can respond in several ways. If you don't notice or ignore me, I will feel rejected and will be less likely to reach out for support. Even worse, if you notice but are condescending in response: "Of course you are overwhelmed—you are incompetent," I would never want to reach out for support or trust you in the future. But if instead you notice and respond in a way that demonstrates vulnerability: "I remember how overwhelmed I was my first time doing this—what can I help you with?," once I acknowledge what you said, both of us have signaled and shown that we are safe with each other. The loop is complete, and we can now trust each other at this higher level. Notice that people's signals for support precede the trust. It is because someone puts out a signal that we are willing to trust them, not the other way around. This means that if you want to build a meaningful relationship with someone, you have to be willing to put out a signal. Trying to look perfect is a really effective way to alienate people. This does not mean to overshare; it means risking being vulnerable. At times your signal may go unnoticed or you may feel embarrassed, but most of the time people will respond well and you will feel closer.

For the Marines in boot camp these signals may go beyond a verbal signal or request. Since their daily routines are intentionally overwhelming, it would be impossible for any one person to accomplish everything necessary on their own. They quickly learn that they will either help each other when they see someone struggling or risk the group being reprimanded. Throughout any given day, thousands of these vulnerability loops are created and completed. From making sure people's shoes are shined and everyone is in formation on time to meeting required dress code, the only way to get it all done is to support one another. Even a task as small as getting your own water bottles filled and equipped on time can require the support of another person. The trust that normally takes years to build suddenly happens in weeks. Strangers who couldn't be more different bond so deeply that they refer to one another as family. They have become people who would lay their lives down to protect their fellow soldiers.

Steve's master stroke is in creating a problem big enough to require people to collaborate. The IKEA effect takes hold as countless vulnerability loops are opened and closed, causing trust to increase and people to bond. All of this works because of a little chemical Dr. Paul J. Zak calls the moral molecule.

Dr. Zak has made a career of researching the neuroscience of human connection, cooperation, and corporate work culture. On any given day at his lab, he may be testing groups problem solving or soldiers marching in unison or the effect of tandem skydiving (when you are strapped to another person) on connection. His research focuses on an incredible neuropeptide known as oxytocin.

Many of us know of oxytocin as the cuddle chemical. It gained fame for its effects on bonding mothers with their newborns by flooding the mother's body during and after labor or during the care and feeding process. As researchers learned more about oxytocin, they realized it wasn't exclusive to women; in fact, the chemical rises during any prosocial behavior, from giving a hug to making love.

According to Dr. Zak, intimacy loops are consistent with what we know about oxytocin release. When people complete a loop, the brain will release oxytocin to drive more prosocial behavior. Athletes participating in a team scrimmage will not only feel more bonded to one another but will also demonstrate more kindness and consideration to other teams. Think about it like this: when you get great news, you feel a high and rush of happiness, and suddenly you are smiling at complete strangers and are more open to people. Similarly, an increase in oxytocin primes the brain for trust and interaction. This is why Dr. Zak sees oxytocin as the moral molecule; it signals to our brain that we should care about a person or group. It ensures that we bond to each other and our young, and as a result, we treat one another better. Without it, we likely wouldn't have survived as a species.

It turns out that the effects of this moral molecule can be magnified depending on the situation. In Dr. Zak's lab, when running experiments where groups feel increased pressure, like racing a clock to complete a task, the increase in stress causes higher levels of oxytocin, and participants bond faster. You may have had a similar experience if you have ever been on the single rider line (for people going on rides by themselves) at a theme park. Even though you are surrounded by strangers, the excitement increases prosocial behavior and leads to fast bonding with the people around you. As with most things, when excitement turns into high levels of stress, the effect changes.

Dr. Zak points out that when human beings are under sufficient stress or when they are put into a context in which people see the world as us versus them, increased oxytocin has been found to lead to a division. As you can imagine, if a group is bonded with high levels of oxytocin like those in Marine boot camp and someone is threatening the group, behavior can turn from prosocial to tribalism.

Under these extreme conditions, where the context is life or death, oxytocin may work more like a tribalism chemical than a cuddle chemical. It would explain why people who are in love will feel more connected to everyone, but soldiers about to go into battle will feel bonded only to their comrades in arms. The increased stress and the context of being around enemies will create tribes.

Hopefully, none of us will know the extreme stress and tragedy of battle, but it does help us understand why and how people bond deeply. It also gives us a clear recipe for how to build trust with people quickly.

We finally have all the pieces to the puzzle of Steve's success and the Marines' incredible speed of bonding. Now we have an approach we can use to grow the trust you need with the people who are important to you, whether that is high-profile customers, philanthropists, investors, or even a new social circle that will get you fit. Clearly, at a base level you have to demonstrate your benevolence, honesty, and competence. This isn't a sprint—this is essential over the course of a friendship, career, or your lifetime. Relationships are very hard to maintain if people don't feel that you have their best interests at heart. This doesn't mean you should hide the fact that you want them as a customer or donor, but rather that they feel that you want the best result for them. After all, wouldn't you want a salesperson who protects you and makes sure you feel taken care of or a fundraiser that honors your donation so it accomplishes what is important to you? This is the benevolence that I am talking about.

Now that we have the critical pillars in place, we contextualize our relationship using the halo effect. We demonstrate the common social ties just as Gino does. This isn't about name-dropping but about finding trusted common ground. Ideally this came through a warm introduction, but that wouldn't always be the case. In the Influencers community that I created from the dinner party, only about one or two of the guests at each dinner come by personal recommendation. In those cases, there is a greater sense of trust. Often high-profile people like celebrities and politicians who would never have accepted a random invitation will trust us and attend, and if there is someone in particular I want to meet, and it is never who you would expect (e.g., Peter Cullen, the voice of Optimus Prime from the *Transformers* movies and cartoon), I will find someone who could introduce us.

For the majority of people you will engage with, there won't be a meaningful halo for you or anyone else in the group to build off. In these cases, especially in the business world, people try to impress or win over strangers by pampering them with luxury and gifts, but the IKEA effect shows us that we need to take the exact opposite approach. At the Influencers Dinner we create a problem big enough to require everyone's support. A meal needs to be prepared in less than an hour, and without everyone putting in effort, we don't eat.

Suddenly, everyone is involved, chipping in. With so much to get done, vulnerability loops are being completed at a rapid rate. Within an hour a group that started as strangers is now seated in awe of all they accomplished and eager to spend more time with one another. They have been flooded with oxytocin, and a trust that normally takes months or years to develop is created in an hour. The best part: it was all done with benevolent and honest intentions.

Now that you know the mechanism, you can apply it in your own way. What is absolutely essential is that you use this knowledge in an ethical way. The intention of this book is to enable people from any background to develop deep and meaningful relationships that improve not only their lives but the lives of all those they connect with. Building trust quickly with non-benevolent motives probably will be seen as manipulation, eventually this behavior is discovered, and people's reputations are hurt. The simple test that I will keep bringing up in this book is: If you tell people what mechanism you use and why, would they feel manipulated, and are they okay with it? To be honest, I think someone as good-natured and smart as you, someone who would recommend this book to so many of their friends would by definition be benevolent. I say all of this as a precaution, because what I care about is people developing relationships that make their lives better.

So, what do we take away from this section of the book? For starters, you should ask people for more favors. It will cause them to like you more and strengthen your relationship. It also means that you should stop taking clients out for expensive dinners, and instead find a joint activity like a hike, a fitness class, an art project, volunteer work, or even flower arrangement. The key is that it is something that will cause you to invest effort together and, ideally, is consistent with what you enjoy and value. When you do, you will notice how quickly friendships form, all because of a problem, group effort, vulnerability loops, and a moral molecule.

Connection

Chapter 5

The Problem with Connecting

⸻

O n August 2, 2008, Iggy Ignatius was overwhelmed with joy. All ten of his investors had just handed him checks funding the development of his dream project, a retirement community in central Florida. Within a month, Iggy found himself in the worst economic downturn since the Great Depression. Florida had gone from one of the hottest real estate markets to a historic low. Developers around him were filing for bankruptcy, and people were defaulting on their mortgages. To make matters worse, across the street from his development, four-bedroom houses were selling for $100K, while he was selling two-bedroom houses for $130K. He was in trouble . . . or so he thought. To his surprise, he instantly sold out an entire wing. He suddenly had enough money to build two, and before he knew it, he sold every unit he had. But how was this possible? Iggy's retirement community was charging 30 percent more for half the space. That's like getting 38 cents for every dollar you spent, at a time when Americans had lost much of their money and savings.

The answer lies in Iggy's vision and a collection of biases that guide our behavior. Iggy had immigrated to the United states from India in the 1970s. He was an ambitious man in his twenties looking to build a life, and by the late 2000s that life was filled with a wonderful family, grandchildren, and a successful career. Like many of his friends, he thought of retirement in India but realized that their aspirations to return home would mean leaving their friends, children, and grandchildren behind and giving up the high-quality medical care that the United States had to offer. But what if there was a way to have it all? What if there could be a "little India" in central Florida that provided the culture, food, activities, religious considerations, and community that these people desired so deeply?

For the residents, it would be a little piece of heaven called Shanti-Niketan. This would be a place where everyone understood their accents and food preferences and respected their religious beliefs. It would mean connecting with people who shared the same values and desires for their later years. They would get everything they loved, from rice, curry, and homemade yogurt to Bollywood movies and yoga.

In the middle of an economic crisis, while everyone else was going under, Iggy was an incredible success, all because he offered people something his customers couldn't find anywhere else—the ability to connect with their culture without giving up their connection to family.

Over a thousand miles away from ShantiNiketan sits a laboratory at Northwestern University's Kellogg School of Management, run by famed neuroscientist Moran Cerf. In a collaboration with the mobile dating app Hinge, Moran and I teamed up to understand a different kind of connection—what causes people to connect for dating. In what may be the largest dating study in history, we reviewed the data from over 421 million potential matches. Since people don't actually date on a mobile dating app, but rather connect on the app with the hope of meeting in person, we looked to understand which factors had the greatest impact on whether or not people exchange contact information. I should point out that we never saw any of the users' data, profiles, or conversations.

What we discovered was wildly amusing. First, the old adage "opposites attract" really didn't hold up. Instead, in almost every case, the more similar people were the more likely they were to connect. This goes down to their initials. If people had the same initials, they were 11.3 percent more likely to connect than those who didn't.[1] This phenomenon is known as implicit egotism—essentially anything that reminds us of ourselves is more attractive and appealing. This may sound insane, but researchers found that people named Denis are more likely to live in Denver and become dentists,[2] or after the storm Katrina, girls were more frequently given names that start with "K," like Katherine and Katie, because of the familiarity of the sound from media outlets.[3] With dating, this effect continued to every aspect of people's profiles, from religion (average 97.5 percent increased chance, and a range between 50 percent to over 850 percent depending on the religion) and school type (when both people attended liberal arts colleges there was a 38 percent increased chance; Ivy League colleges had a 64.3 percent increase) to phone use (Android vs iPhone), and even what NCAA conference your college was a part of. This is incredible, but why was this effect so profound? For us to understand this, I will share the story of one of the most daring art heists in history.

On Monday, August 21, 1911, at 6:55 a.m. a man dressed in a white workman's smock entered the Louvre Museum of Paris, France. Every Monday, the Louvre was closed to the public for cleaning, maintenance, and logistics, allowing the man to wander unnoticed. As an added benefit, on these days the museum staff went down from an already skeletal security team of 166 to a meager group of 12 to patrol what was the largest building in the world at the time (1,000 rooms across 45 acres). As the man walked through the empty halls, he entered the Salon Carré, a room featuring Renaissance paintings. Once inside he briefly pondered which of the many works by the Italian masters appealed to him the most, and for the purposes of the escape, simply grabbed the smallest. It was an unremarkable work, but with the frame removed, it was a convenient size to escape with. He hoped to carry it out of a side door and leave unseen, but on this day the side door was locked, and he needed an alternate plan. So he did the unimaginable: he wrapped the painting in his white smock, tucked it under his arm, and walked out the same way he entered.[4] Amazingly, no one noticed, and no one thought to stop him. It wasn't until the museum opened to the public the next day that an attendee reported a missing piece to security.

The museum security assured the person that the piece must have been removed by Louvre personnel to be photographed or for restoration, but eventually it became clear that they had been robbed. Newspapers around the world picked up the story, some even as a front-page headline, not because anyone had ever heard of or cared about this obscure work painted in the Italian Renaissance, but to poke fun at the French government's incompetence in managing the Louvre. As outrage of the theft increased, and reward money was offered for its return, this unnoticed piece hanging in a side gallery of the Louvre quickly became the most famous painting in the world.

The heist was legendary, and when the Louvre reopened, people flooded the Salon Carré, among them famed author Franz Kafka, just to see the empty spot where it once sat. A total of 6,500 wanted posters were distributed across Paris to help the public identify the painting, and with pressure mounting to catch the thief, sixty detectives were assigned to the case. They tried to track down leads or clues, but nothing was emerging.

Then, two months later, someone in search of reward money came to a local paper claiming that they had stolen works from the Louvre several times and sold them to their "friends." It didn't take long for police to realize that the "friends" being mentioned were the poet and writer Guillaume Apollinaire and a Spanish artist named Pablo Picasso. Yes, the very same Picasso who was soon to be the world-renowned cubist painter. When word got out, the two realized that they had to dispose of the stolen art. They packed everything in a case and under the cover of night headed to the river to toss it in, but in that moment, they couldn't bring themselves to do it. Instead Apollinaire returned the work to the local newspaper, asking for anonymity. A few days later police detained him and ordered Picasso to appear before the magistrate. The two men were terrified; Picasso in his panicked state even claimed to have never known Guillaume. In a stroke of luck, the works they had returned were not a Renaissance painting but Iberian sculptures made in the third or fourth century BCE. In fact, these pieces were the inspiration for Picasso's famed painting *Les Demoiselles d'Avignon*.[5] Having nothing to do with the theft of the painting, the case was dismissed, and the two were off the hook.[6]

It wasn't until December of 1913 that the painting appeared again. After having stored the painting in his apartment for more than two years, Vincenzo Peruggia, a glassworker and craftsman who worked at the Louvre, boarded a train to Florence and met with a famous art dealer to sell it. But once the work was verified, the dealer called the police, and Vincenzo was arrested. After pleading guilty, he served a meager eight months. Meanwhile, the world rejoiced at the return of the painting. It was taken on a brief tour of Florence, Milan, and Rome, and then returned to the Louvre. Now that it was the most famous painting in history, when this portrait of a woman painted by Leonardo da Vinci was rehung in the Salon Carré, over one hundred thousand people came to see it. It was protected by bulletproof glass, guards, and the best security system money could buy. Da Vinci's *Mona Lisa* now attracts more than eight million visitors a year.[7]

So how is it that an unnoticed painting from 1507 that wasn't even recognized by art critics as a valuable representation of Renaissance work until 1860 could go from almost irrelevant to what many consider the greatest painting ever made? And what does it have to do with ShantiNiketan, and how we connect and even date?[8]

An interesting quirk or bias we all have is that just being exposed to something—a food, a sound, a product—will cause us to like it more. Have you ever noticed that sometimes when you travel it can be challenging to try the local cuisine? If you have ever tried Vegemite, a yeast extract popular in Australia, you will notice that locals swear it's the best snack, but foreigners, to put it mildly, find it less than ideal. Or maybe when a new song came out, you just weren't into it, but then the tenth time you heard it, it started getting good. This is what researchers call the mere exposure effect. We are wired to like, trust, and feel more comfortable with something the more we are exposed to it. The reason the *Mona Lisa* is a legendary painting is not because it is vastly superior to all others, but rather that we have all been exposed to it so many times, and the only reason we were exposed to it to begin with was that it was stolen. Chances are if it hadn't been stolen, we would never have heard of it, and it would still be sitting on the wall of a side room in the Louvre instead of attracting millions of photos and selfies.

The mere exposure effect is so powerful it has an impact on what we eat, how we dress, and who we spend our time with. Amusingly, the one thing we are exposed to more than anything is ourselves. So, it stands to reason that those people who share the most in common with us would have the most potential to connect with us. Which explains why people were willing to pay so much to live at Shanti-Niketan. This is also why in our study on dating we found that across almost every characteristic (initials, college type, NCAA sports conference, religion, etc.), the more people had in common, the more likely they were to connect.

If we are honest, most of us don't connect with people who are substantially different from us. We tend to spend time with people who have similar political views, income levels, religious beliefs, favorite sports teams, and so on. You might say something like, "Mike is a member of a different religion and we are best friends." Although there can always be outliers, chances are if you look at Mike's income, career, political views, values, and sports teams, there will be a lot of overlap with yours. These are known as multiplex relationships. A single plex would be a relationship that has one commonality (e.g., you are a customer at a store and the other person runs the register). If you two also use the same hairstylist, go to the same gym, and attend the same church, then you two have multiple points of relatedness and you have what's called a multiplex relationship. Research has found that as the number of points of contact increases, so are the chances that people are connected. This shouldn't surprise you, considering that each additional plex offers more exposure. What may shock you is the incredible effect of distance.

If every time we wanted to hang out with a friend we needed to drive six hours, chances are we simply wouldn't. In the 1970s Thomas Allen, a professor at the Massachusetts Institute of Technology, wanted to understand what effect distance between offices had on people's communication or connection. Clearly, if someone is in another country, you probably won't ever meet, but how often do you connect with someone at work if you have adjacent desks as opposed to sitting across the floor from them? When graphing the frequency of communication versus desk distance, Allen found a surprising result. Communication grew exponentially the closer two people sat. If two people were separated by more than fifty meters, their communication began to disappear. This relationship would later be known as the Allen curve, and it holds up for digital communication as well. As Allen said in his book:

> **our data show a decay in the use of all communication media with distance. . . . The more often we see someone face-to-face, the more likely it is that we will also telephone that person or communicate by another medium.**[9]

This is the reason ShantiNiketan was such a success. After a lifetime of being exposed to the same culture, politics, food, and religion, they had a community packed with multiplex relationships and proximity. It was an environment in which everyone could naturally connect without any effort. As the adage goes, it allowed for birds of a feather to flock together. Their similarities drew them to congregate. These stories should give you some insight into how you ended up with the friends you have. Chances are they look like you, participate in the same activities, and live nearby. It may also explain why you went down the career path you chose. I'm often amused by how many children do similar work to their parents; it is, after all, what they were exposed to.

Having this common ground may be comforting when you want to reminisce about your favorite childhood shows or watch the local sports teams, but this is incredibly limiting when you have aspirations and goals that extend past your inner circle or where you grew up. What we want is a way to connect with people beyond these limiting factors. We want meaningful relationships with the people we respect, admire, and can add to our success. In my case, I didn't grow up with billionaires, professional athletes, celebrities, or business executives. If I were limited to who I grew up with, I would mostly know creative people, as my father is an artist and my mother is a musician. As inspiring as that may be, it had nothing to do with what I wanted to learn or what career interested me. But now my life is infinitely richer because of the diversity of my relationships. I owe that to all the time I spent researching how to go beyond the mere exposure effect and multiplex relationships.

It began with the realization that to connect with people, regardless of their level of influence, we need to understand two essential elements:

1. What will get them to notice us? No one will take a meeting, buy a product, or donate to a nonprofit they don't know exists, and a student won't pledge at a sorority they have never heard of.

2. How do we entice these people to want to engage with us? Even if they have heard of us, our product, cause, or organization, they need to see enough value to spend their money or be involved.

Answering these questions will allow us to connect with whomever we want. Remember, before someone meets us, they probably don't know who we are or how wonderful we are. From our perspective it's hard to imagine that they wouldn't want to be a part of our social circle, but the fact is that in order to connect with most people we need to understand what they value. Remember, it was when Jean Nidetch provided people with what they cared about—a healthy lifestyle—that she created a connection, and her community formed. So, while others ask what they can get from people using a self-serving approach, we will take a benevolent approach and focus on what they care about.

Chapter 6

How to Connect with Anyone

———

W hen I was twenty-eight sitting in that seminar, I realized that if I wanted to connect with influential people, I
needed to understand what they value. I knew that with
enough effort I could figure out how to meet almost anyone, but the
goal wasn't to just shake someone's hand once and get a selfie. Instead
I wanted to develop meaningful relationships. I wanted the people I
admired to be a part of my social circle or community and for them
to connect with each other. The problem was that I didn't grow up
around important people, which meant I didn't understand their
lives or what would appeal to them. So, being the geek that I am,
I went out and interviewed assistants, business leaders, and friends
who could share insights with me.

What's obvious in retrospect is that people's motivations differ
drastically. Some are driven by social impact, others by wealth and
power, and yet others by having someone attractive to flirt with.
Even if I had the time or interest to research each person individu-
ally, chances are I would get it wrong because we often don't realize
what our own motivations are. Instead, I looked to understand what
commonalities influential people have, but I learned that treating all
people who have influence the same would be like treating children
of all ages the same. Any parent can tell you that four-year-olds and
teenagers have different interests. Similarly, important people differ
in who they influence and how, and as a result their lives, social pressures, and what they value vary drastically.

I needed to find a way to group people and then figure out how
to connect with each group. Initially it wasn't clear if it should be

by industry (technology, media, etc.), audience (churchgoers, Free-masons, sports fans, etc.), or something else. I came to see that as the scale of someone's influence changed, so did their social pressures. This may seem obvious now in a world where people relate to influence based on the number of followers a person has on Instagram, but in the late 2000s Instagram didn't exist and influencer wasn't a career.

I was able to separate people into four groups:

1. *Global Influencers:* These people have a reach that spans across the world, which means they have an ability to impact economies, get instantaneous press attention, and are internationally known. Although most earned their status through business and political efforts, some, such as royalty and celebrity, can attain it without. Examples: Queen Elizabeth, the president of the United States, Elon Musk, Oprah Winfrey, Sir Richard Branson, Bill Gates, Beyoncé.

2. *Industry Influencers:* Members in this group have the ability to impact their industry and have earned its respect through their thought leadership (professor, scientist, author, etc.), positions (CEO, CMO, editor-in-chief, general, etc.), or previous success (sold a company, earned an Olympic medal, Nobel Prize, Oscar, Grammy, etc.). Notice that while a global influencer is often recognized outside of their industry (everyone recognizes Richard Branson), most people can't name the CEOs of the top ten companies in the Fortune 100 even though each of those leaders has an incredible influence in their industry.

3. *Community Influencers:* The level below an industry is a niche or a community. At companies it might be holding a position of VP, where a person is accountable for a significant organization, budget, or result. It may be as a spiritual leader, sen-

sei, or instructor serving a religious or cultural community. Alternatively, these people could be creatives who have garnered a large following but have yet to reach industry-level recognition. Put simply, they can impact or guide a community or niche within an industry.

4. *Personal Influencers:* The people who impact your life and vice versa are your personal influencers. They could be your best friend, your family, your coworkers, even your hairstylist, schoolteacher, or trainer. The important part is that it is a two-way relationship. This is not someone you solely follow on social media; it is someone you connect with.

Once I was able to separate people out into these four groups, I could then research what they valued and how to connect with them. But let me point out that there is a big pitfall we need to watch out for. While there is nothing that would make me happier than to learn that you are developing relationships, people often focus too much on connecting with famous people, thinking that the more important the people are the better. Don't get me wrong, it can be very cool and sexy to hang out with celebrities and big names, but in most cases, that's probably not going to help you with your goals. At least not the ones that really affect the quality of your life. If you want to develop the relationships to get your child into a good school, knowing Mark Zuckerberg probably won't help much. In this case, connecting with a community influencer like the school's dean or leaders in education would have a bigger impact. The important takeaway is that it isn't necessarily better to know global influencers than industry or community influencers. One group is not better than another. What matters is what you want for your life, career, company, or cause.

I didn't want to limit my relationships, so I needed to understand what each group valued. The approaches I developed are designed to not only facilitate connecting with people but for them to connect with each other. We want everyone to be better off and to feel like we are all part of a healthy social circle. In the pages ahead I will provide a strategy for each group. I encourage you to read them all and then choose which one works best for what you are looking to accomplish.

Chapter 7

Connecting with Global and Industry Influencers

W hen I ask people, "If you could meet any living person, who would it be?" the answers tend to depend on the person's age. My thirteen-year-old niece, Aydin, probably would say Trevor Noah and Taylor Swift, but adults' answers tend to be names like Elon Musk, Oprah Winfrey, Warren Buffett, Angela Merkel, Sir Richard Branson, Beyoncé, Jeff Bezos, and Michelle Obama. Your list might be different—it may include more athletes or politicians, maybe a celebrity or two. Whether your ideal person to meet plays football, is a banker, or sings in a band, there is a good chance they are internationally or at least industry famous. What is surprising is how different the social pressures are for global and industry influencers, and as a result there is a difference in approach and philosophy for each. Since almost everyone has a dream person (often a global influencer) to meet, we will begin with them and then explain how they relate to industry influencers.

Global Influencers

Global influencers are in such high demand that they often have private security, executive assistants, managers, agents, chiefs of staff, and full teams in place to get their work done. As a result, they tend to live in a bubble. From the moment they get up to the moment they go to bed, every part of their day is scheduled. Sometimes their team will be in their home in the morning so they can get started right away and then will travel with them from meeting to meeting, all with little or no contact with the outside world. From home to car, to meeting, to car, to plane, to car, to hotel, and lunch meetings, work, family, and everything in between, they are managed and whisked off to make sure their busy schedules are fulfilled.

Even if you were able to get into an event they are at, you would then need to get past their assistant, security, and team in a respectable way. That would be no small challenge. Of course, if you happen to be a global influencer yourself, you could just have your team reach out to schedule some time together or you could score an invitation to an ultra-exclusive event like Google Camp, which was dubbed by the media as a "billionaire summer camp."[1] In 2019, it made headlines for bringing President Obama, supermodel Karlie Kloss, and designer Diane von Furstenberg together with the likes of Katy Perry, Harry Styles, and an ever-growing list of industry icons.

If you prefer less sexy but more secretive, you can find your way to the Bilderberg Meeting, where every year since 1954, 130 politicians, financiers, and thought leaders meet[2] in secret to discuss topics concerning North America and Europe. I'm not going to lie—that sounds like the plot of a James Bond film.

Possibly the best known of these events is run by the World Economic Forum, which engages very high-profile political, business, and cultural leaders to shape global, regional, and industry agendas. These business and political leaders meet for a week in January to enjoy the cold of Davos, a small town in the Alps of Switzerland. Essentially, if you are lucky enough to get invited to buy a $50,000 to $210,000-plus ticket to attend, you will have the privilege to hobnob with the CEOs of global companies, billionaires, prime ministers from around the world, the president of the United States, and thousands of others.[3] So, unless you have a spare billion hanging around or happen to run the International Monetary Fund, we are going to need a different approach. I found the solution for connecting with these global influencers in an unexpected place: the New York theater world.

Scott Sanders had a vision. After producing countless shows at New York City's famed Radio City Music Hall, he wanted to create a show that could redefine the Broadway audience. To put it into perspective, in 2004 less than 4 percent of all Broadway attendees were African American, and most of them probably attended a single show, *The Lion King*. Sanders's idea was to bring the Pulitzer prize—winning novel *The Color Purple* to life on stage. In order to attract a new audience, he wanted the support of someone everyone loved and trusted. He wanted Oprah, who was in the film adaptation in the 1980s. As you can imagine, someone as famous and respected as Oprah can be hard to get a hold of, and Sanders would need hours of her time to see the show and talk about it.

Instead of reaching out to Oprah directly, he used what I call the "ubiquity approach," and the best part is that he did it unintentionally. Global leaders tend to have a tight-knit circle of trusted friends, business partners, and employees. They may be lawyers, accountants, and agents, they may run divisions of their companies, or they may even be best friends. The ubiquity approach is simple: if you connect and develop a trusted relationship with people in their inner circle, in time you will become a part of their community and you will be pulled in as a trusted member. After all, if you are friends with the presidents of Tesla, SolarCity, SpaceX, and Neuralink, it won't be long before you are hanging out with Elon Musk. You will notice that this inner circle is often made of industry influencers.

So, Scott took his time. Over the years he was developing the show, he would find himself at Oprah's studios in Chicago working on projects with industry leaders like Diana Ross and Queen Latifah. With Oprah thirty feet away, he had to restrain himself from interrupting her with a cold pitch. He knew that he needed a warm introduction to be taken seriously. As the show was entering a final workshop, he asked his coproducer, music legend Quincy Jones, for his suggestions on how to get press. Jones suggested he reach out to Gayle King, who not only worked at Oprah's magazine at the time but was also, to Scott's surprise, Oprah's best friend. When Gayle accepted the invitation to see a preview of the show, she found it so compelling and brilliant that she texted Oprah: "Scott is doing you proud."

A few days later, Oprah called Scott and sight unseen asked to invest. As you can imagine, Scott was flattered, but what he was really interested in wasn't money. He wanted to have a place on Broadway where the African American community could come and feel represented and, in the process, attract more than a single-digit audience of color. A few months later when the show's marquee was put up, it displayed "Oprah Winfrey presents *The Color Purple*." Her seal of approval got people's attention, and the show's compelling adaptation of Alice Walker's book was able to keep it. It both became an unstoppable hit and fulfilled Scott's dream. Fifty percent of attendees were African American. Scott knew that Oprah's involvement meant the show would attract people who wouldn't have likely attended a Broadway play, and it worked.

Years later Oprah told Scott that if he had approached her when he was in her building a year or two before they were introduced, she would have felt that he wanted too much from her. The fact that Gayle invited her to meet him, when he was ready to launch, allowed her to bring her secret sauce and audience. Getting brought into a global influencer's inner circle by a trusted person makes all the difference.

Even with all Scott had going for him as an industry leader, he took his time to make sure the relationship developed in the right context. The lesson here is simple: take your time to build relationships with industry influencers and only then find a way to connect with global personalities.

Experience tells me that although this process is effective, it is not always as satisfying as we might expect. For starters, the real joy of connecting is developing lasting relationships. People who operate at a global level don't necessarily have the bandwidth or interest to be pulled into our social circles or community. This isn't to say they wouldn't love being involved; it is more that they have so many responsibilities that it is often not realistic. Let's be honest—I doubt the Queen of England is shopping around for a new best friend. The more important point is that depending on what you want to accomplish, the people in their inner circle can probably handle it better than they can themselves. If you want Sir Richard Branson to work with your cause, you are probably better off connecting with the head of his nonprofit Virgin Unite. Not only is that person easier to reach and develop a relationship with, but they know the day-to-day priorities and intricacies of what can and can't be done. In the time it would take to reach Richard, you would be able to connect with twenty organizations like Virgin Unite. Since the people in global influencers' inner circles tend to be industry influencers, let's take a look at how to connect with them.

Industry Influencers

When Richard Saul Wurman planned the first TED Conference, it was an unmitigated financial disaster. He had hoped it would be like hosting the "ultimate dinner party," but in 1984 people may not have been ready for his ideas. He believed that audiences were tired of conferences, and that they didn't want to hear another old white guy in a suit drone for an hour about how great his company was. Instead he would take inspiration from the Bauhaus design movement that emphasized simplicity and function. Richard thought he would remove everything not essential from conferences. He subtracted panels, suits, lecterns, long speeches, PowerPoint, introductions, and countless other little things that no one would miss. Eventually, all that was left was a single brilliant idea, an idea that could be delivered in eighteen minutes or less.[4] This would be an "anti-conference," a place where he could assemble the best and the brightest, and unlike almost every other conference in the world, a place that was not limited to a single area of interest (e.g., medicine, computing, architecture). Instead, he would bring people together from across industries with a focus on technology, entertainment, and design (where the name TED comes from). To make it even more unique, like many of the best dinner parties, TED was invitation only.[5]

Richard's style was wildly different than anyone could have expected. He would stand on stage with the presenters, and if they bored him, he would stop them and send them off. Since the talks were short, when someone was great, it delighted you, and if they weren't, they disappeared before you got annoyed. Even with incredible presentations by leading minds and demonstrations of cutting-edge technologies of the time, like the compact disc player and e-book reader, the conference lost a fortune.

It would take another six years until Richard and his business partner tried it again, and this time the world was ready.[6] In the days before social media and viral marketing, TED would sell out a year in advance.[7] It was, and remains, one of the few places you can rub shoulders with award-winning musicians, billionaires, architects, writers, Nobel laureates, inventors, and the like all in the same place. Richard eventually sold the company to Chris Anderson, who converted the organization into a nonprofit and led its incredible global expansion. In 2006, at the suggestion of June Cohen, the then director of TED Media, they began to post the talks online.[8] In the years since, TED has become a global entity with conferences in multiple continents, partnerships with some of the biggest brands in the world, and offshoots known as TEDx that are run independently in hundreds of cities around the world.

A lot of organizations attempt to create extraordinary conferences and events, but why is it that TED eventually succeeded? Part of the answer had to do with Richard's idiosyncratic leadership style, the conference's unconventional format, and, of course, the specific cultural moment when it was launched. But there are additional timeless qualities that we can learn from and reproduce in our own effort to connect with and influence others.

When I began to research the lives of the industry influencers, the type of people we see at TED or an Influencers Dinner, I realized just how much people want from those operating at the top of their industry. Specifically, what people want falls into five categories I call their STEAM: status, time, expertise, access, and money.

It's naive and perhaps even arrogant for someone to think that they can just walk up to an industry leader at a conference or email them with a request and get a positive response. Industry leaders are inundated with requests and have learned to filter them carefully. But, through my research, I've identified four qualities you can cultivate to get your interactions and events to be more compelling and sustainable: generosity, novelty, curation, and awe.

These four qualities have been found to consistently get the attention of industry influencers and draw them in. Generosity, novelty, curation, and awe are what create a desire to connect on a deeper and more meaningful level. I should point out that you don't have to have all four all the time, but the more of them you include the greater your chances of having industry leaders want to engage. It will be up to you how you prioritize them.

Generosity

What is generosity? Is it giving someone a gift, helping them move, or donating to charity? What makes you generous is that you give more of something (e.g., money, time, product) than necessary or expected. You might hear that and think we need to shower people with gifts, but that's not what I'm talking about. To understand this idea, let's explore the research of famed Wharton professor Adam Grant. Grant examined the success rates of medical students, salespeople, and engineers, and within each group compared people who are givers (generous), takers (those who exploit), and matchers (those who mimic behavior—they give back to givers but don't give to the takers).

When comparing these three groups, Grant found something surprising: the people with the lowest grades in medical school, lowest incomes as salespeople, and lowest productivity as engineers were all givers. Now that seems to go against everything I have been preaching so far. How is it that caring about other people and wanting to contribute reduces your success?

It also begs the question: Who are the most successful individuals? Oddly, the most successful are also the givers. Grant noticed that what separates the givers who succeed from those who fail is knowing where to draw the line. Those who give more than expected to the point they can't take care of what they need to can experience burnout. If you are a medical student who helps everyone else study, but you don't leave enough time for your own studies, your grades will suffer. On the other hand, if you can give more than expected and make sure to take care of yourself at the same time, you will have the support of not only other givers but also the matchers. So why is it that givers tend to be at the top? Grant explained that takers tend to rise quickly and fall quickly, since the matchers, looking for a fairness of sorts, will call them out for being exploitative. In fact, companies with a giving culture operate better across every possible metric from profits and customer satisfaction to better employee retention and lower operating expenses. This is the kind of healthy generosity that is our sweet spot. We need to balance generosity that welcomes people and lets them feel included with making sure we succeed and don't experience burnout.

One of Richard's master strokes with TED was the way he integrated a generous spirit into the entire experience. It was clear that Richard's main objective wasn't to make money off people, but rather to bring them together for something special. Being a part of such a high value community is extraordinary, and then if you're lucky, he'd give you the stage. It is an opportunity to share an idea with the industry leaders you admire and respect most and let you shine. TED's generosity comes from the fact that the community's contributions brought it to life. It works because people give more than is expected of them, and they receive more than they expect. No one is paid to speak, and people are honored to attend and participate.

This is a key distinction; people frequently confuse generosity with gifting. Brands and often people try to win others over with lavish experiences, high-priced products, and event gift bags at parties. When asked what they do with those gift bags, most people will tell you that they rarely if ever keep anything. Unless someone is already a fan of the company or product, they usually either throw them out or regift them, even high-priced items like cell phones, computers, and appliances. Remember, Benjamin Franklin didn't win over his rival by giving him a book but by getting his rival to go out of his way to bring a book to him. Similarly, we need to focus on the kind of generosity that gives people the opportunity to invest joint effort, feel included, and create connection. That is how we create a foundation of trust in which people will receive more than they expect. It is this kind of generosity that the Influencers Dinner is built around. We give people an invitation that allows for a joint effort and connection. You may invite people to go on a city hike or participate in a workshop, sport, or art project. It has even been proven to work with collaborative team video games.

Unfortunately, generosity alone is rarely enough. Industry influencers get countless invitations to attend events and receive free products, so we need to go past generosity and look at what else can get their attention.

Novelty

Allen Gannett, author of *The Creative Curve*, would argue that things appeal to us when they are original enough that they are interesting, but also familiar enough that they are safe. If it is too familiar, it is cliché and uninteresting; if it is too different, it becomes uncomfortable or avant-garde and only appeals to a niche. It is the reason we all know the name of Iceland's most famous musician, Björk, but probably don't listen to her music on repeat. It is the balance between being new and familiar, and it likely has something to do with a section of the brain known as the SN/VTA (substantia nigra/ventral tegmental area). This is what researchers refer to as the "major novelty center" of the brain.[9] When we are exposed to something new or different, the SN/VTA responds proportionately to how novel the thing is, and here is the important part for us: it "entices us to explore and understand it." Meaning, when something is new and different, we are drawn to see it and understand it. But, similar to the creative curve, if something is too novel, like alien spaceships landing, we would get scared and avoid it. The key is to find that sweet spot. For most of us, the challenge will be making what we do more novel, although there are some of us who come up with ideas so crazy we will need to reel them in.

There is a simple test to know if something is novel enough. Ask yourself: "Is it remarkable for the right reasons?" Meaning, is it worthy of being noticed for being extraordinary or uncommon? For generations, our species has passed down our knowledge through oral history. If something was important or culturally relevant, people would remark about it. If it wasn't remarkable, it would be forgotten. If you want influential people to notice and engage with you, something needs to stand out for the right reason.

The old newspaper adage that "if it bleeds, it leads" demonstrates this paradox. Violent stories capture our attention easily, but they are remarkable because they are shocking and upsetting. We need to stand out for the right reasons, ones you want to be associated with.

We can see this principle play out in a very healthy way at TED. Since the conference isn't limited to a single industry, people are exposed to brilliant thinkers across every possible field, and the talks are designed to be understood, regardless of your level of knowledge or expertise. Suddenly ideas are cross-pollinated between industries. Whereas before, you would have to hear hours of lectures or read hundreds of pages to be exposed to an idea, Richard's speakers give you a personal master class in a few minutes on a topic you never knew existed. Once Chris Anderson and June Cohen started putting the videos online, these industry titans started speaking to the world.

Did it pass the remarkability test? Without a doubt, to the tune of hundreds of millions of video views. Not only did people watch, but they shared, and the public loved it so much that viewers volunteered their time to translate the best talks to other languages so the entire world could learn and be inspired.

If you have ever watched a TED Talk, you will notice they aren't sensational, they don't preach the end of the world, and they rarely discuss violence, but they are novel, and so was Richard's format and how Chris evolved it to a global platform. Novelty can be created from amazingly simple characteristics. At the Influencers Dinner guests can't talk about their careers and most TED Talks are limited to nine minutes. One of my favorite examples is the Six-Word Memoir project, popularized by Larry Smith. Inspired by Ernest Hemingway, the idea is to tell your life story in six words. A couple examples: "Moved every year then came home" by Allison Harris and "Her dreams kept her reality warm" by Lisa Anne Pottle.[10] Mine could be "Dyslexic screwup, wrote book, showed them!" Notice how simple these examples are. They don't require huge amounts of effort, although if you are inspired to create something big, go for it. The point is that the results trigger curiosity and are worth talking about. The best part is that most novel experiences don't require investing a lot of money. Richard could have tried out TED's format in a living room at no expense before he put it on stage. When I started the Influencers, there was no rental equipment, staffing, or expensive foods. It was just a group of people and a format that stood out.

Curation

Who do you think the most influential people in our culture spend the most time with? The most common answer I get to this question is either "other influential people" or "their family." Then I remind them how much time important leaders spend with their admin or executive assistant. This is the person who manages their schedules, lets them know where to go and when, and makes their life work. After their admins, they speak to their teams, clients, maybe their boss depending on the company, and, at the end of the day, their family or friends.

The fact is, they would love to meet other influential people just as much as you would, and so they are happy to travel great distances and spend huge sums of money to attend Davos, the Milken Institute's Global Conference ($15,000 to $50,000), TED ($5,000 to $50,000+), and the like all for a chance to hear interesting ideas (although you can often hear and see those online for free), and, more important, to meet and spend time with exceptional people. Although there was a reduction in gathering in physical spaces after COVID-19, there was still a high value placed on being in the "right" Zoom room or virtual event.

When we consider attending an event, whether it is social or professional, our first question typically is: "Who is going to be there?" Let's be honest, we don't want to hang out with boring people or people we dislike.

The more influential a person is, the more demands they have on their time. This is why industry influencers are willing to travel and spend to ensure that they walk into a room full of the people they want to meet. Like a great museum curator selecting the right combination of art to display, our job is to select both the people in a room and in our social circles and communities. To be clear, I'm not saying you should cut people out of your life or that each relationship needs to be calculated, but it is important that you have the right mix of people. In an ideal situation, everyone there is excited to meet or talk to at least one or two others. If everyone wants to talk to the same person, the gathering will feel out of balance. It also doesn't mean you need to have a lot of people—often the right three or four people can be far more enjoyable than two hundred. In any great gathering of people, there will be more who want to participate than there is space for attendees. This isn't exclusivity for the sake of pretention, like a nightclub trying to seem cool by keeping people out. Rather, the risk is that as people are added, intimacy breaks down and the ability to bond on a meaningful level tends to diminish. Our objective is to both develop and grow relationships and have people connect with each other. Curation is about filling the spots with an interesting mix of people so that everyone enjoys themselves and is better off.

Since Richard saw TED as the ultimate dinner party, he would invite guests so that every person in attendance could be the person on stage. Such a high standard ensured that everyone was interesting and well worth talking to. The diversity of the guests' backgrounds and expertise only added to the value and novelty while reducing competition and hierarchy. This is the same thing that happens at the Influencers Dinner: the Tony Award–winning theater professional is not competing with the Pulitzer Prize–winning photographer or the Olympic athlete. They are each fascinated by and have a profound respect for each other.

This isn't to say you need this kind of diversity. You may want to create a greater connection within a specific community (e.g., school-teachers, cybersecurity experts, writers, marketers). Regardless of your ideal community, you want to make sure to curate effectively.

Awe

Arguably the most desired human emotion or mental state is awe. Not because love, happiness, and belonging aren't wonderful, but because awe is so rare. It can be described as "an overwhelming feeling of reverence, admiration, fear, etc., produced by that which is grand, sublime, extremely powerful, or the like."[11] It causes people to reposition themselves in the universe. These are rare moments, like when a parent holds their child for the first time. They might say something like "The universe disappeared around me, and it was a perfect moment, just the two of us."

When people experience awe, they report feeling more generous and connected. Triggering this feeling to some degree is an incredible context to build a relationship from.

I want to emphasize two things. The first is that this is an incredibly high standard to meet. I don't expect awe to occur often, but including it as a principle causes us to think to a higher standard. The second is that awe is not the same as novelty. We don't experience awe every time we try something new. Instead, an awe-inspiring moment causes a sudden shift in perspective that allows us to see the world in a new way. We experience the grandness, the interconnectedness of life. Something that was impossible or unthinkable before becomes a new paradigm.

People who watched the Moon landing, attended the first Macintosh demo, or even the first time they went to a planetarium and saw how small we are in the grand scheme of things have experienced awe. Novelty is much easier to produce, and the effect is generally temporary. Awe, on the other hand, is something we rarely forget and can cause our perspective to shift. It may be triggered by a stunning vista, an inspirational piece of art, or even looking into a microscope to view the smallest forms of life in existence.

During TED, these moments happen occasionally. A scientist sharing a discovery for the first time, a technologist demonstrating unpredicted breakthroughs in technology, or an artist sharing a feat of creativity. It's hard to imagine the world without the technologies we use every day, but on the TED stage in 1984 they demonstrated the first e-reader, more than twenty years before Amazon's Kindle was released. These kinds of moments would cause a fundamental shift in thinking from an audience spanning countless industries.

We have moments at Influencers Dinners when people are left speechless or dumbfounded. It doesn't happen at every dinner, but when it does, it is unforgettable. When participants find out that the person they made guacamole with is a Nobel Prize recipient or a twelve-time NBA All-Star, they get a look on their face of wide-eyed confusion and disbelief. It is really wonderful.

As you consider what you want to create, ask yourself how you can trigger awe. This is a near-impossible standard, but when you can achieve it, people will come from far and wide to connect and be inspired.

Industry Influencers: Putting Generosity, Novelty, Curation, and Awe Together

Clearly there were many reasons Richard and then Chris were able to turn TED into a success, but what we can learn from this example is that there is a definitive and timeless set of pillars or values that will get industry influencers to connect. If you create an event or experience that has one or even two of these characteristics, you can have a hit. If you manage to combine three or four of these pillars and it is organized and designed well, you will have a home run.

If you want to be noticed by and connect with industry influencers, you need to create something new that stands out. You want to ask yourself:

1. *How can I be generous or create a space of generosity?* It doesn't need to involve you spending lots of time or money to run events. It could be as simple as hosting a potluck or starting an online forum on an important industry topic. What's most important is that what you are giving has a value worth them investing effort. We want to make sure they care, and that the IKEA effect kicks in.

2. *What novelty can I bring?* If what you have is a copy of another event, it won't stand out and won't trigger their curiosity or attention. If it is novel enough, it will be remarkable, and people will talk about it. The novelty can come from the format, the food, or what people bring, talk about, or do once they are there.

3. *Who are you curating?* Are you connecting within an industry, at an intersection (e.g., technology and film), or across multiple industries? Even when our consulting practice helps companies to develop industry-specific communities, we often

suggest including a few people from neighboring industries (e.g., researchers to share ideas, journalists to tell the stories). This ensures there are people who members don't already know from years of working together.

4. *How can you trigger awe?* This is by far the toughest principle. Sometimes it can happen through surprises, new ideas, or communing with nature. Don't get too caught up with this, but it doesn't hurt to ask yourself and other people and search around.

In addition to the Influencers Dinner, my team and I have developed countless other experiences for both the Influencers community and our clients. One of the most popular is Inspired Culture: The Salon by Influencers. After most of the dinners we host an additional sixty to one hundred community members for cocktails, and about an hour in we surprise them with three twelve-minute presentations sharing new and unexpected ideas from scientists, artists, and celebrities and performances by musicians or magicians. Our speakers have ranged from Bill Nye the Science Guy and two-time Grammy award winner Rahzel, formerly of the Roots, to legendary architect Bjarke Ingels, musician Regina Spektor, and numerous Olympic medalists and Nobel laureates. After the talks, guests mingle and are free to discuss anything. By 2020, I was hosting three of these salons every month across New York, Los Angeles, and San Francisco. Notice the simple structure manages to be generous, novel, well-curated, and, with the right topics, awe-inspiring. This serves to continue to bond the community after they attend a dinner.

Now that we have an understanding of how to connect, I want to take a moment to look at who we should focus on. Trying to create a comprehensive list of potential guests can be overwhelming. To make the process more manageable, we apply what is called Price's law. The physicist Derek Price noticed that if you look at all the work being published in the sciences, half of it is produced by the square root of the contributors. That means that if there are twenty-five authors of scientific papers, five of them have done half the work. If you want to create a Hollywood entertainment community, we begin with the four hundred thousand people working in the industry. We take the square root, and according to Price's law, about 632 of them are probably doing half the work. It is why we keep seeing the same actors', directors', and producers' names everywhere. Making a list of six hundred people is a much more manageable task than reviewing four hundred thousand people. I'm not sure if this law works in every industry, and there are probably a lot of people who would be ideal for you to connect with but didn't make the list, but it does let us narrow down the pool of people you want to engage with.

Regardless of who you are trying to connect with, keep your expenses extremely low and your logistics minimal, especially at the beginning. At the same time, try to host people who are supportive and will give you honest, constructive feedback.

Whatever you create, make sure that it meets at least two of these four criteria. Look for opportunities for people to contribute while also making it possible for those who give to get value in return. Look for ways to break the mold—for people to do something they never tried before or to take a well-established genre and mix it up. Be selective about who participates—both who leads and who follows, who speaks and who listens, who teaches and who learns. And program your events and experiences to make space for moments of surprise and awe. And one final note: whatever it is you create, be sure it's something that you would enjoy being part of too. Think of yourself not just as the organizer but as a participant. The same four elements that apply to others apply to you. Are you being generous? Are you learning or doing new things? Are you excited to meet other participants? Are you awed and inspired by the experience? The fact is if you don't enjoy it, you aren't going to want to keep doing it.

If you don't have any ideas right now, don't worry about it. We have plenty of time and a lot left to cover.

Chapter 8

Connecting with Community and Personal Influencers

———

I am often asked if we can use the same strategy to connect with community leaders that we used for global influencers in the previous chapter. The simple answer is yes—who wouldn't want to have a generous, novel, well-curated experience? But the strategy for global influencers is designed to address their social pressures; since community influencers have different social pressures, using a mismatched strategy may prevent us from reaching as many people as we want. By definition there are more communities than there are industries, and so we need an approach that has the potential to work at a larger scale. Interestingly, this approach also has the potential of having the biggest impact on the people closest to us. So, we begin by looking at how to connect with community influencers and then those we care about most.

Community Influencers

It's funny to think that Dietrich Mateschitz was a traveling toothpaste salesman, especially since he was someone who dreamed big. His latest idea, launched in 1984, was to bring a soft drink known as Krating Daeng to Europe. He had gambled his life savings on the reformulation,[1] but on first impression people would describe it as tasting like "carbonated cough syrup" and "mildly reminiscent of urine."

Even after the negative reviews and losing more than a million dollars on the project, he was undeterred. Most entrepreneurs in his situation would either shut down the project or focus on celebrity endorsements in hopes that the increased buzz and exposure and the halo effect would convert into sales and popularity. After all, earlier that year, Pepsi signed the biggest star in the world at the time, Michael Jackson, as their spokesperson for a then record $5 million.[2] It was a tried-and-true equation for success. Unfortunately, Dietrich didn't have that kind of money, but what he lacked in finances, he more than made up for as a brilliant marketer.

Without the budget for a significant marketing push, the company became a master of guerilla tactics. Among the more brilliant ideas was creating brand curiosity by throwing empty cans on the floors of nightclub bathrooms. After all, if you see it there, it must be illegal or against the rules, which made it seem mysterious and exciting. They launched partnerships with liquor brands and even leveraged the fact that they were banned in some countries to make people want the beverage more. When the World Wide Web soared in popularity, they created a rumors section on their website to spark conversation, but what is most relevant for us is understanding how they captured the attention of community influencers.

In 1997 Dietrich was finally ready to bring his drink to the United States. He partnered with Many Ameri and Torsten Schmidt, the German cofounders of cultural consulting and marketing agency Yadastar. Their theory was simple: if you want to create true brand loyalty, you need to integrate into communities and add value. While most brands spend wildly to put their names on stadiums, concerts, billboards, and the like, Yadastar argued that it was more important for a brand to form a deep and lasting connection with community members. Superficial sponsorships might offer a bit of influence from the halo of the event or even give you a time slot on stage, but people see through that. It doesn't create a relationship between communities and the brand, and it absolutely doesn't give consumers a sense of the brand's values.

Instead of sponsoring a festival, they started a small music academy. In the days before convenient online forms, people submitted handwritten applications and sent in CDs of original music to be considered for the two weeks of training. In the first year, they received three hundred applications from three countries, and just sixty students were selected. There were beat producers, record collectors, jazz musicians, MCs, engineers, musical virtuosos, singer-songwriters, DJs, and everything in between. During the day, Torsten and Many brought producers and creators from all corners of the musical universe. During their free time, the attendees were encouraged to take their inspiration into an onsite recording booth to collaborate on new music.

The music academy was an instant hit, and over the years as the academy's reputation grew, so did the status of the creators who spoke, including legends from Erykah Badu to Ryoji Ikeda, Pusha T to Werner Herzog, Björk to A$AP Rocky, Nile Rodgers to Ryuichi Sakamoto, all for a modest honorarium. As a graduation gift, alumni were given an original T-shirt with the brand logo on it. This was a company that at the time made no swag, so owning this shirt was a sign of status; it meant you had earned your stripes. Then when the musicians went on to perform in front of crowds of thousands, they wore the T-shirt with pride. When interviewed by the media, they thanked the brand, and as they grew from community influencers with local followings to industry leaders, they represented the brand because the music academy helped them grow. This is part of the reason you know the Red Bull brand and logo so well.

During the course of more than two decades, the Red Bull Music Academy received over 80,000 applicants and trained more than 1,000 students from 120 countries. As a truly respected member of the music community, Red Bull was able to grow the academy into an ecosystem of local workshops, studio sessions, and events in more than sixty countries. Most notable of those events is the Red Bull Music Festival, the critically acclaimed series of month-long city festivals that celebrates great music, music culture, and the transformative minds behind it in nineteen cities around the globe. These real-life projects were complemented by signature channels for in-depth music journalism, including the 24/7 radio station Red Bull Radio, a long-form written editorial hub, podcasts, print publications, books, films, and more.

Over the years, Red Bull has made many brilliant marketing moves, but it was the shift from product-oriented marketing to authentic involvement in the music community that led Red Bull's transition from a caffeinated sugar water to one of the most valuable lifestyle brands in the world and the envy of Madison Avenue marketers. Whereas most brands have to pay media outlets to reach an audience, Red Bull owns the outlets and the direct connection to their ideal customers. This incredible brand relationship and status allows it to be one of the most expensive liquids in the world, and Dietrich sells more than 7.5 billion cans a year.[3] That's more than one for every person on the planet.

This same playbook was what led to the Red Bull Flugtag (German for "flight day" or "airshow"), an event that can only be described as completely insane. During the Flugtag, people are invited to design and build a human-powered flying machine, transport it to the location, and launch it off a pier to see how far the machine can fly. You might think that would be something like a science fair with groups of engineers competing, but in reality it is far more creative and ridiculous. Popular entrants have included a giant rubber duckie, a stork holding a baby, a giant puffer fish, a *Star Wars* X-Wing, a four-legged dragon on wheels, the car from *Ferris Bueller's Day Off* (it went off backwards like in the movie), a giant roller skate with wings, a cardboard fire truck with no wings, and so on. None of these contraptions was really designed to fly—they mostly just fall directly into the water, creating a glorious splash and massive applause from the upward of two hundred thousand people in attendance.

So why is it that Yadastar and Red Bull succeeded where so many others failed so embarrassingly to connect with communities and their leaders?

The answer lies in understanding the mentality of community influencers like the up-and-coming artists who were accepted to Red

Bull Music Academy. They have tasted some success, but chances are good they don't yet have the know-how to get to that next level. Even if operating at an industry level doesn't appeal to them, developing mastery or working on exciting projects often does. The academy gave them four critical assets:

1. *Skills:* The refinement of their abilities (e.g., presenting, managing, working with teams, or even industry-based skills like DJing and painting).

2. *Opportunities:* To know about and be able to apply to or participate in unique projects or experiences. These are rare chances to prove oneself and demonstrate skill and competence to increase their reputation (e.g., a chef cooking for a famous food critic, a comedian opening for a big name, a musician getting to be heard by a famous producer).

3. *Access:* The ability to meet industry leaders or attend highly selective gatherings and locations.

4. *Resources:* What people need goes beyond just money; it could be a recording studio, experts, supplies and materials, or transportation.

In essence, we need to help them SOAR (support them with skills, opportunities, access, and resources), and that is exactly what Torsten and Many did with Red Bull Music Academy. They provided a support system to help these musicians take their careers to the next level. They trained them, made introductions, shared knowledge, provided recording studios, and countless other things. And they hired them to perform at the Red Bull Music Festival. They were able to nurture their careers, not by sponsoring them but by being there with them, understanding what they needed. In a very tangible way, they added value to people's lives.

In 2019 when it was announced that Red Bull Music Academy would be closing, both alumni and the media were sad to see it go. The music magazine the *Quietus* wrote: "For all the complexities it reflected, [RBMA] created something of lasting and deeply personal value, an antidote to the depersonalized aggregation of music and culture embodied by Spotify, YouTube and others."[4]

What Yadastar and Red Bull created was truly extraordinary. Most companies aren't willing to invest the time in a strategy to help others SOAR, but when they do, sponsorship money that would typically be given to another company to grow their brand can be used to create a direct relationship with the communities they care most about. Instead of slapping their name on a banner as a sponsor of festivals like Coachella or EDC, Red Bull was able to authentically enter the music media industry to create their own festivals and media outlets worldwide.

It is important to note that for a large and established company it will take more time and effort to develop relationships with community influencers. Since companies come and go with sponsorship money, it can take time to establish authenticity on a large scale. On the other hand, if you are an individual or small company, there are fewer preconceived notions, so showcasing your authenticity is easier, and you don't need as large a scale to impact brand perception.

As I mentioned earlier, this isn't the only strategy that will work. Community influencers will be drawn in by a generous, novel, well-curated, and awe-inspiring experience, just like industry influencers, but not necessarily the other way around. The difficulty is that even when industry leaders are looking for skills, opportunities, access, and resources, their needs are much more specialized the further they are into their career. It might work if you focus on one industry, but I have yet to see it done well across industries. The added challenge of using a SOAR approach with industry influencers is that they can often hire around whatever they lack. If they don't have a skill or access, they bring in a consultant, agency, or new staff member. Regardless of which strategy you choose, they each have their strengths.

You will notice that many organizations use the SOAR approach, from MBA programs attracting students to take their career to the next level to the Weight Watchers commitment to improving health. In any case, the promise is that through participation you will have what you need to redefine your future. If this is the strategy you want to apply, you don't have to make the significant investment that Red Bull did. You can begin with small gatherings and get a sense of what people need most. In time, you can develop a format in which you or fellow participants teach each other and share knowledge, outside speakers are invited, or even an online platform like Craigslist develops.

Personal Influencers

It probably won't come as a surprise to you that the most challenging group to influence can be those closest to us—our personal network of friends and family. Sure, they may take our recommendations on which phone to buy or what restaurant to try, but when we suggest that they need to exercise more or quit smoking, they often resist our perfectly reasoned and researched arguments for why they should change. I am not saying you should give up on them, but you may need to take a different approach.

In Chapter 1, we learned the profound impact that our social circles have on behavior. Just knowing someone who is obese, depressed, happy, a smoker, or even voted in a certain way increases our chances of taking on those characteristics. Behavior and habits are contagious. So instead of focusing on persuading that person to take our advice, consider trying to connect them to others who have a skill or habit you'd like them to adopt. Instead of guilting or manipulating someone into doing something, encourage healthy friendships with healthy habits. This approach has the highest chances of succeeding if a person is a community influencer, someone who is respected and actually lives by these values. Changing a habit, a lifestyle, or a mental model is hard no matter what. And it isn't enough to simply introduce your father to a doctor who tells him to exercise—most of the medical doctors I know don't take their own advice. The person needs to live the value or characteristic you care about, and they will need consistent contact. With enough of these relationships, you can create a community of positive influence, and your chances of affecting change increase considerably.

So far we've focused on how to build trust and connect with those we respect and admire. Now it's time to turn to the third part of the Influence Equation: how to develop a sense of community. By getting people to participate in an engaged and vibrant community, our relationships become stronger and the positive impact on everyone's life increases. We want to go beyond simply connecting to make sure your relationships grow over time, and for that we need to understand what gives us a feeling of belonging.

Sense of
Community

Chapter 9

The Structure of Community

———

Now we get to explore one of my favorite topics: giving people a sense of community. That same characteristic that we learned in Chapter 2 that is so crucial for living a long, happy, and healthy life is also critical for succeeding in our careers, raising children, getting fit, and anything else we care about. Regardless of who you want to connect with, if it's an intimate group of five or ten people or a national grassroots movement of twenty million people, our goal is to create deep and meaningful relationships. It is the difference between taking a fitness class and feeling like you are a member of the fitness community. It gives people a sense of belonging.

As you consider what you care about and who you want to connect with, my biggest suggestion would be to make sure you focus on something you really value. You don't want to hang out with a lot of scuba divers only to find you hate swimming. Regardless of whether you join an existing community and become an active member or foster one developing around you, being a part of something that you truly care about will have a profound potential to positively impact everyone involved.

Being able to connect based on our personal interests hasn't always been easy. For most of human existence, our communities were defined by geographic distance. If you lived in Rome two thousand years ago, you wouldn't be part of the same community as those who lived in what's now South America. Neither group even knew the other existed. There was no platform or place where a community made of Romans and Mayans could come together. Only once we entered an era of fast transportation and communication could we find people with similar interests. In time, we began to see communities grow beyond proximity and into areas of interest, like professional communities (unions, guilds, associations, etc.), hobbyists (ham radio operators, bird watchers, etc.), fan groups, religious affiliations, and so on. People became members of organizations ranging from the Girl Scouts of the USA and National Geographic Explorers to fraternities and competitive drone racing leagues. When we become an active member of a community, we experience a sense of belonging, like we are where we are supposed to be. What is amazing is that thanks to technology you don't even need to be on the planet to participate. An astronaut near the Earth's orbit can log on to a website like Reddit to answer questions and connect with a community of space enthusiasts and amateur rocket engineers. People who one hundred years ago would have never found a place can now connect from anywhere to find their community both locally and globally.

It is this feeling of belonging that we want to nurture and develop. There is an important distinction that we will keep coming back to. Notice I didn't write "belonging" but rather the "feeling of belonging." It is our feelings that are our test for reality, and we will consistently act based on how we feel. This is why people don't just have a desire to be in a community but also desire that experience of feeling at home. It is what psychologists David McMillan and David Chavis described as "a feeling that members have of belonging, a feeling that members matter to one another and to the group, and a shared faith that members' needs will be met through their commitment to be together."[1]

As we have discussed, this feeling of belonging has a profound impact on every aspect of life and seems to function like an idyllic cure-all for whatever we care about. For instance, women with breast cancer are four times more likely to survive when they are part of a large network of friends versus those that have a sparse group of friends.[2] Employees who feel connected to each other are more productive and healthier and their companies are more successful. Social movements tend to have a greater long-term effect than an individual protest. So, what is it that gives us a sense of community? This was the question researchers McMillan and Chavis were trying to understand back in 1986. They identified four characteristics that are necessary to foster a true feeling of belonging:[3]

1. *Membership:* There are those who are on the inside and those on the outside.

2. *Influence:* The community has an impact on the members, and the members have an impact on the community.

3. *Integration and Fulfillment of Needs:* The needs of the member and the community are aligned so that both get value.

4. *Shared Emotional Connection:* There is a shared participation and history or journey that members are on.

To understand why these characteristics are important and how they apply to us, we will visit South Africa, Wikipedia, a US prison, and one of my favorite places, a haven and heaven for geeks: Comic-Con.

Chapter 10

Membership

———

In 2003, the Springboks, South Africa's national rugby team, was
in shambles. Their performance in the Rugby World Cup was,
to put it mildly, embarrassing. To make matters worse, the team
was in the midst of one of the biggest scandals in rugby history. In
an incident known as Kamp Staaldraad (Afrikaans for Camp Barbed
Wire),[1] players were taken for a "team-building" experience that involved getting naked together in foxholes while ice water was poured
on them, crawling in gravel, and killing and cooking chickens (but
not eating them).[2]

In 2004, Jake White was brought in as the new coach. Unlike many
coaches before him, White didn't come up from coaching professional provincial teams; instead he got his start coaching high school
rugby, then was the assistant coach for the under-21 national team.
When he took over as coach, the team won the under-21 Rugby World
Cup. Now, as the coach of the national team, he was playing with
the big boys, and I mean big. John Smit, the man he selected as team
captain, was six-foot-two and 268 pounds, and Smit wasn't even the
biggest guy on the team.

White had only a few years to prepare the Springboks for the 2007
World Cup, but he had a simple plan. First, he targeted the players he
thought were capable of leading the Springboks to success and built
the team around them. Second, in a wildly uncharacteristic move for
a professional sports team, White told his key players that they didn't
need to worry about the short-term results, that they had safety in
their position. Finally, he instilled a total belief that they could and

would win the 2007 World Cup. White was unwavering in his commitment to prepare and train the team to take home the Cup.

In interviews team partners explained that one of White's greatest skills was recruiting and hiring people who complemented his personality. No matter what White's strengths and weaknesses were, his assistant coaches and captain did their part. As a result, the culture the Springboks developed could be described as the creation of a brotherhood. This was an interracial team, less than twenty years after the end of apartheid, and White, his assistant coaches, and his captain, Smit, made sure everyone was included. Whereas many teams end up splitting into camps based on provinces, politics, race, and so on, the Springboks had no place for division. White picked his core team, he trusted and stood by them, and he protected them in the media, no matter what. This gave them a sense of safety and belonging. In return, they fought as a team, and the results were immediate. Out of the gate, they went on a four-game winning streak, which eventually built up to a stunning and unexpected win of the 2004 Tri Nations Series (their first since 1998). Their incredible comeback led them to earn the World Rugby Board Team of the Year award.

The following year, 2005, the Springboks came back in full force but lost the Tri Nations on bonus points. The next year, 2006, was a tumultuous one, marked with five consecutive losses (six in total) in a nine-game season. They had countless injuries, surgeries, and even a broken neck. After all, rugby is not a sport for the frail. Even as the critics bashed White's decisions to hold on to his core group, he never lost faith in his players and continued to play them. To give you a sense of White's loyalty to his players, the Springboks were readmitted into international rugby in 1992 (after the end of apartheid). As of writing this book, only six players have ever achieved centurion status (playing one hundred or more tests, which is rugby for match), and five of those players were White's core team. White was so loyal to his core team that he would play them regardless of criticism or short-term results,[3] even though the typical strategy is to replace older and injured players with those who are younger, fitter, and faster.

Since his first day as coach, White had been preparing the team for the challenges they would face in 2007. Not only would there be another Tri Nations Series, but they also would be competing in the Rugby World Cup. They started the Tri Nations strong, but the core team was injured and worn out. The South African Rugby Union released a medical report stating they "cannot risk their remaining stars ahead of the World Cup."[4] Without their star players, the Springboks came in last.

No matter what the critics said, White held true to his priorities. There would be another Tri Nations next year, but the World Cup only happens every four, and South Africa had something to prove. His job was to protect his boys and make sure they didn't just play, but that they won and remained healthy. With critics berating him in the media, the question loomed: Would White's faith in Captain Smit and the core team prove the right move for the World Cup?

The 2007 Rugby World Cup brought twenty international teams to France to compete. The Springboks made short work of their initial matches, earning them a spot in the quarter finals to face off with Fiji. Unfortunately, it was not as easy as Springboks player Jaque Fourie had told the media it would be. With fifteen minutes left, the score was tied, and Fiji was fighting hard. Smit called the team together and reminded them to get their heads in the game or they would end up eliminated. The team rallied and took the lead, winning 37–20,[5] giving them the opportunity to face and defeat Argentina in the semifinals.

On October 20, 2007, the Springboks took to the pitch (rugby term for field) to go face-to-face with England. Tensions were high, as White and his coaches had put everything into building this brotherhood. But were they the right group or should he have selected younger stars even though they would be less familiar with each other? His critics would look at this test as either proof that White deserved their harsh criticism or that the team were heroes of South Africa.

Both teams fought for every inch, but eventually the Springboks scored and were able to take and grow the lead. When the clock ran out, the Springboks became the 2007 champions of the Rugby World Cup. What John Smit remembers most about that winning moment wasn't the screaming and cheers but the intense relief. Just a year before, they had lost five games in a row, and by all accounts he and much of the core team should have been replaced, but White wouldn't even consider the idea. He would remain faithful to his team. In the end, White had proved himself to the critics and the fans and would be returning home as one of the most iconic coaches in rugby history.

Considering that a few years earlier the Springboks were an international embarrassment, what was it that had them coalesce into a World Cup Championship team?

When speaking to some of the Springboks' partners, they point to White's ability to masterfully create a sense of community. White himself may not have been close with each individual player, but his coaches and Captain Smit understood how to bond them into a brotherhood, giving them a sense of community.

As I mentioned in the previous chapter, a sense of community is built from four characteristics, with membership coming first. Membership means the right to belong. It is the feeling that you are welcome in the community, you are at home. This separates members from non-members. The Springboks' leadership accomplished this not just through continuously playing the core team, but from the brotherhood that formed between the players. Membership breaks down into five characteristics: boundaries, emotional safety, a sense of belonging and identification, personal investment, and a common symbol system.

Boundaries

In order to feel like you belong to a group, there must be clear distinctions between those on the inside and those on the outside. Some communities wear uniforms (the Girls Scouts, sports teams, the military), others require a website login (Reddit, Wikipedia, Facebook), while others just require you to show up (book clubs, AA, meetups). Without boundaries you can't feel a sense of community because there is no clear identifying characteristic that bonds people. White's boundaries extended past uniforms and showing up; he was wildly loyal to his core team, playing them year after year regardless of results. You can create boundaries in simple ways. Just naming an activity can give it a boundary that differentiates it from everything else. I don't host a supper club; I host the Influencers Dinner, and now I have member or dinner alumni. It is important to note that if we push boundaries in the context of unhealthy competition or intense fear, it can have negative results. It is not unheard of for sports fans from opposing sports teams to fight or groups to become violent with outsiders. You want to make sure that your boundaries foster healthy interactions and develop a great reputation for the community.

Emotional Safety

People cannot feel that they belong if they are threatened or worried their opinions will alienate them. As we saw in Chapter 4, the ability to be vulnerable is a critical element for any group, community, or team dynamic. If members cannot voice their concerns, make suggestions, or bring up opposing opinions in a safe way, the community or team is more likely to fail. White made it clear that he would protect his players and would not judge them by short-term results. By Captain Smit's own words, he should have been replaced a year before the World Cup. Imagine how far you would go for a leader who protected you like that. When you host or assemble people, what can you do to have them feel safe and welcome? Will you greet each attendee personally? Do you welcome all new participants as a group or ask someone to be their host and show them the ropes? It doesn't need to be complex. In our emails we include frequently asked questions to make sure they are clear on everything and understand the etiquette. That's one of countless little signals we give to make sure they know they are welcome and can ask anything.

A Sense of Belonging and Identification

This is the feeling that you are part of the group and that you describe yourself as a member. It is the difference between saying "I go to a church sometimes" and "I am a member of a church" or saying you work at a company and talking about the company as "we." In one you are an outsider who visits, and in the other the group is part of the way you self-identify. The Springboks' leadership developed a culture in which they were one team. There were no camps within the team, and everyone had a sense that they were welcome and a feeling of acceptance. There was a fundamental expectation of belonging. Some companies have a culture in which Legal is going against Marketing, Manufacturing is causing problems, and so on, but when anyone from any title can connect with anyone else, there is a true sense of belonging. If you want people to self-identify, you may want to define a term. Within the AA community members self-identify as "I am a friend of Bill," referring to one of the founders. Since we never want to encourage or be the cause of unhealthy behavior at Influencers Dinners, we may quietly ask, "Are you a friend of Bill's?" This allows us to be respectful and discreet and we'll know not to offer them a drink.

Personal Investment

We have discussed this principle a few times: when a person invests effort (the Ben Franklin or IKEA effect), they care more and they feel a more profound connection. The sorority sisters from Chapter 4 invested huge amounts of effort during pledge week. The Springboks dedicated their lives to represent their country on the pitch. I would encourage letting people invest effort and provide support. It will allow them to feel more connected to the group and have a greater feeling of membership.

A Common Symbol System

When doctors speak to each other, there is a common medical language. This internal communication system exists across any kind of community, from secret handshakes at fraternities to words and symbols in online groups and personal jokes between you and your friends. Any group that trains together as many years as the Springboks will have a culture of phrases, shorthand, and jokes that are part of the inside group. On top of that are the actual symbols that represent the group. Sororities have their Greek alphabet, companies have logos, countries have flags, and so on. As you develop your group or community, you may want to develop a logo or symbol.

These membership cues have a way of telling you, "You belong here. You are safe, welcome home." Once someone is on the inside, we want to give them an opportunity not only to be influenced by the community but also to influence the community's development in a positive way.

Chapter 11

Influence

———

It was an argument over identity. It began as a heated discussion over whether it should be a capital *I* or lowercase *i*.[1] The advocates on each side shared the intricacies and justifications of their views. At times they were respectful and cordial, and occasionally it would devolve into childishness. Each side's philosophical and technical arguments would have made Socrates himself both swell with pride and cringe with disappointment, but they argued with passion because it was something that mattered to them and would represent what they cared about to the world. When the dust settled, it had taken two months and over forty thousand words[2] (that's about five thousand more than you have read so far in this book) before they were able to come to a conclusion that made no one happy. The Wikipedia page for the movie *Star Trek Into Darkness* would be written: "*Star Trek into Darkness* (usually written as *Star Trek Into Darkness*)."

You may have missed it because the difference is so subtle and frankly would be irrelevant to almost anyone, but the argument was whether the word *into* should start with a capital or lowercase letter. Yes, you read that right. In almost the same amount of writing as F. Scott Fitzgerald's classic novel *The Great Gatsby* (47,094 words) and Douglas Adams's *The Hitchhiker's Guide to the Galaxy* (46,333 words)[3] was the equally engaging and page-turning argument about capitalizing a letter in a reference site about a film.

If it isn't already absurdly clear, I'm a geek. I love *Star Trek*. In fact, I love the entire franchise, and I love that people spent hours on this debate. Even though I wouldn't enjoy spending my time arguing about it, this corner of the internet is home for those who do care, and I am happy they found it and each other.

The page eventually updated to *Star Trek Into Darkness*, possibly after an anonymous user posted "READ THE GODDAMN OFFICIAL WEBSITE, YOU POMPOUS IDIOTS."

What I love about this story is that it demonstrates that we can find a community that cares about almost any topic. Chances are the people who argued about this Wiki entry are passionate about at least two things:

1. *Wikipedia Accuracy:* Incredibly important considering how many people turn to the site for answers.

2. *Star Trek:* Equally important considering how much I like the show. Okay, maybe not equally important, but I'm the one writing the book, so can we agree on "very important"?

The debates demonstrated the second characteristic of a sense of community: the importance of influence. As I mentioned in Chapter 1, influence is the ability to have an effect on an outcome or person. For people to have a sense of community, it is important that they can both contribute to and be affected by the community. Influence must flow both ways.

If you can't contribute, then you can't have influence, and the relationship only flows in one direction. A one-directional relationship is not a community; it is an audience, fan, or follower. This is what differentiates someone with a large social media following or a media outlet where the influence is mostly one-directional from your local knitting group or parent-teacher association meeting. On this Wikipedia page, anyone who felt it was important could contribute their perspective, and they did to the tune of forty thousand words. And as they interacted within the community they were exposed to other people's perspectives and hopefully were able to expand their thinking. Influence was at play in both directions.

While this example may sound ridiculous, if we are honest all of us have interests we obsess over that really only interest us or a small number of people. The only difference is this one was public and amusingly wild.

In most cases people's influence is more subtle, such as a conversation with a coworker, doing volunteer work at a religious center, mentoring a student, or sharing ideas. The acts don't need to be grandiose; they just have to represent a give-and-take.

Chapter 12

Integration and Fulfillment of Needs

―――――

It had been over a year since Coss Marte had seen a doctor. He entered the waiting area and sat next to a man in his early seventies. After his physical exam, the doctor sat Coss down for an uncomfortable conversation. His unhealthy eating and lack of exercise had finally caught up with him. At five foot eight and 231 pounds, Coss was morbidly obese. If he didn't start caring for himself immediately, he would be dead in five years. The doctor then pointed to the seventy-year-old man in the waiting area and said, "You may be twenty-four, but that man will probably outlive you if you don't take care of yourself."

Unfortunately, Coss's career didn't really promote a healthy lifestyle. Coss grew up on the Lower East Side of Manhattan in the 1980s, before it was gentrified. His mother, a Dominican immigrant, worked at a sweatshop and was barely able to cover food and rent. So Coss learned to hustle. He collected cans for nickels, washed cars for a couple of bucks, and ran errands. He was a natural entrepreneur, and sales was his calling, specifically selling what you may call "pharmaceuticals." At the age of thirteen he started dealing weed, which escalated to cocaine and crack, and within a short time his delivery business was running twenty-four hours a day. As the neighborhood gentrified in the early 2000s, his customers became doctors, lawyers, and judges, and his delivery service spread across the tristate area. By the age of nineteen he was doing over $5 million in business and taking home $2 million a year. He had so many customers, he needed seven different phones to store all their numbers (phones back then maxed out at 1,500 contacts). He spent his days sitting in his car eating and drinking and collecting money. It was no surprise he was so over-weight.

At the age of twenty-three Coss's business took a hit when the DEA showed up and arrested him. He was charged as a drug king-pin, which wasn't surprising, since he was moving more than fifty kilos of cocaine a year. Coss was convicted and sentenced to seven years in prison. A year after his imprisonment, he was finally able to see a doctor only to find out he was probably going to die.

Desperate to make a change, he would walk loops every day when the prisoners were given two hours in the yard. On day one, all he could do was walk, but a couple of weeks in, he was able to jog a bit. After a month and twelve pounds lost, a fellow inmate named Bus (five foot six and 310 pounds) came to him asking for help. Bus was diagnosed with diabetes and was a few years away from a coronary unless he turned his life around. Coss started to train with him every day, and as weight came off, more and more inmates joined them. Within a few months, Coss was a healthy 160 pounds and was training a group of more than twenty, who lost a combined weight of over a thousand pounds. The group's comradery was incredible. As a testament to the community fitness training, Bus competed in the Upstate Prison Weightlifting Competition and came in first place after squatting over six hundred pounds.

Coss was doing so well that he was accepted into a special six-month prisoner rehabilitation program. If he could stick with the program, he would be going home a new man, more than three years early. In what seemed a lucky turn of events, with two months left before release, the program gave him access to a dentist. As he entered, a guard demanded to search him. In a show of force, the guard pushed Coss against the wall, causing him to fall to the ground. As he stood up and faced the guard, the guard set off an alarm. Six more security people rushed in and beat Coss to the ground. He was charged with attempted assault and sent to solitary confinement.

Alone in "the box," Coss paced back and forth, knowing that this incident would mean he would have to serve the remaining three and a half years of his original sentence. In desperation, Coss wrote a letter explaining his side of the situation, only to realize he didn't have any stamps. His only possession in solitary was the bible his sister gave him. He lay there depressed, trying to figure out what to do next, when to his surprise, a letter arrived from his sister suggesting he read a passage from his bible.

Coss was not a religious man. The only reason he had a bible was that the guards couldn't take it away and he could make notes in it. Out of boredom, he opened the bible to the passage his sister suggested, and then came Coss's miracle: a stamp fell out. Coss took it as a sign to read the bible from cover to cover, and as he did, he began to think of all the people he'd hurt and all the families he'd addicted to drugs. He had to make it right, but he didn't know how. He was a felon, locked in solitary confinement. Even if he did get out, chances were no one would hire him. To make matters worse, he only knew two things: how to sell drugs and how to exercise with other convicts. And that's when he realized how he could turn his life around and be a positive force in the world.

Coss sat in solitary day after day developing ConBody, a fitness program that trained people the way he trained prisoners in the yard. Not only would he get people fit, but he would educate them on the inequities of the prison system. And he would only hire those who were formerly incarcerated as trainers to help them find stable work. The idea was brilliant, but he was unsure what his future held.

Coss was given an offer: if he pled guilty to the charge of attempted assault, he would be readmitted in the program but would have to start again. Instead of serving three and a half years more, it would only be six more months. Even though he felt it was unjust, he accepted, knowing that this would be the fastest way out. Coss made it through as a model inmate, and six months later he was sleeping on his mother's couch, spending his days talking to any stranger who would listen, inviting them to work out with him twice a day in the park. As ConBody gained followers, he took over a dance studio and hired a former convict from the workout group. When they outgrew the dance studio, Coss opened a dedicated space and hired more trainers. Eventually brands like Marriott and Saks Fifth Avenue started approaching him to open up ConBody locations in their hotels and department stores.

Since its inception, ConBody has trained thousands of people, helping them get fit and educating them on social justice issues in the prison system and the discrimination experienced by felons. The company teaches people that just because someone was convicted of a crime doesn't mean they can't be a contributing member of society. As of this book's writing, Coss has hired forty-two formerly incarcerated felons and none have returned to a life of crime. This is an amazing achievement given that the American prison system has a 44 percent recidivism rate, and for some crimes it's almost 80 percent. This makes ConBody one of the most effective parole work programs in American history.

Throughout his journey Coss has been able to create a true sense of community, initially with his fellow inmates in the yard and now with his instructors and customers of ConBody. The community thrives because it integrates values with goals and needs. People participate because what the organization stands for is what they care about.

Being accepted as a member of an elite military unit, academic program, fraternity/sorority, or even the board of a company carries with it a high status. Being a ConBody trainer means that you have turned your life around and you are serious about staying out of prison. The status of being involved doesn't need to be as grandiose. Being a Girl Scout isn't an elite position, but it does represent that you care to grow and develop. Comparably, whatever you create could simply represent that you value having fun, human connection, education, protecting the environment, or anything else.

Community can offer a demonstration of competence. We wouldn't seek legal help from someone who hasn't passed the bar exam or eat at a restaurant that hasn't passed a health inspection. Similarly, if you are a ConBody trainer, I know that you are reliable, effective, and able to engage with people. These qualities are important for starting a professional organization.

The strength of communities comes from shared values that benefit the members. Professional communities promote and protect careers, sports groups love the game, and religious communities have shared spiritual beliefs. No matter where you look, the values of communities align with their members. In Coss's case, whether he was training in the yard or the gym or working with people on parole, it was clear they were there to accomplish something: to prove that today they can be better than they were before. As you develop relationships and a sense of community, it is important for people to understand what values you stand by. A social movement, a company's culture, and a sports team have very different objectives. In each case, by having clear values, it becomes easier to understand who should be a member, and ensure that their participation is enjoyable.

Ultimately, being in a community means being on a journey together. If our goals don't align, we are on different journeys, and if our values don't align, we will never agree on how to get there. That's why strong communities have an alignment of values and a fulfillment of needs.

Chapter 13

Shared Emotional Connection

———

When Gareb Shamus graduated from college with a degree in economics, he had two problems: he wasn't really sure what to with his degree and he had no idea what to do with his life. The good news was that eventually the degree found a home hanging in his childhood bedroom between a giant poster of the Incredible Hulk and another of Spider-Man. The bad news was he was also staying in that room. Until he could solve the second problem (what to do with his life), he would be living at his parents' home. To thank them, he helped out at the family comic book shop. The year was 1990, and being a comic book fan wasn't considered cool yet. At the time, only geeks and nerds knew who the Avengers were or had ever heard of Marvel, but all that was going to change because of this unemployed, quiet, geeky kid living in his parents' home in the suburbs of New York City.

In his first week at the shop, Gareb noticed that customers kept asking when issues were coming out and about the value of their old comics. It gave him an idea. With the simple publishing software on his new Macintosh computer, he created a weekly newsletter about the comic book industry, offering insights and prices. His little side project quickly grew in popularity, and over the next few months he hatched a plan to start a magazine about comic books for fans like him. By July of 1991, at the mere age of twenty-two, Gareb became the publisher of the magazine *Wizard: The Guide to Comics*. The magazine soared in popularity. For the first time, fans spread out across the world could learn about their favorite artists and storytellers, discover trends, and hear news about toys, films, cartoons, and the

TV shows they obsessed about. In the back half of the magazine, he and his growing team included a pricing guide so collectors could finally find the value of every comic they owned.

Gareb had created a central hub for comic book fans, and hundreds of thousands of people subscribed. Remember, this was before the internet, so a subscription meant people had to pay a fee every year to get a magazine delivered to their home. You might think that with no internet communities, the comic book conventions were where fans gathered, but they were mostly comic book sellers with back issues peddling toys and memorabilia and a few artists signing covers. If they were lucky, the biggest conventions would attract a few thousand people who would each pay $10 to attend. They weren't anything like the celebrity-packed marketing and cosplay events we have grown used to.

In 1995, Gareb decided to "try something crazy." He wanted to throw a massive party for people who loved the comic book world. So, in the same daring fashion that led a twenty-two-year-old to publish a magazine, a now "much wiser" twenty-seven-year-old decided to buy the old Chicago Comicon and transform it. Before the age of cosplay was the age of masquerades, a classic style costume party, but in the world of *Wizard*, those with the best costumes would be featured in the next issue. Millions of people around the world would see these articles and pictures, and while the word "cosplay" had been virtually nonexistent, suddenly it was a legitimate form of creativity.[1]

Over the course of the decade, their innovations continued as they found more ways to include the wide varieties of fan communities and their interests. Thanks to the magazine, Gareb and his team were connected to the toy makers, video game producers, film studios, and marketers. Suddenly he was merging worlds and bringing in the glamour and high production values of the entertainment industry. They created professional celebrity photo ops and meet and greets, video game activations, film promotions, and marketing pop-ups. With every innovation, larger groups came and more communities connected. In time, they expanded to more than sixteen cities and the communities flocked. In the meantime, the magazine gave fans year-round access, expanding their experience from an annual event to a culture they were a part of.

By the late 1990s, the comic book industry was in a slump. Marvel was forced to file Chapter 11, and in 2000, the company brought in a new president to turn things around. Before the new president even started his new role, he called Gareb to talk about the future of Marvel. While most people in the industry sat in offices writing, drawing, or managing, Gareb had a unique perspective. Not only was he connecting with people across all the related industries, but he was engaging with the community of fans every day through conventions and magazines and understood the intricacies of the subcultures.

Gareb joked that after years of writing, the comic book stories had aged characters up so much that the next issue of *Spider-Man* would be *Peter Parker vs. the Prostate Exam*. The fact was that many of Marvel's characters were no longer contemporary or socially relevant. If they wanted to connect with new fans, they needed a reinvention, and Gareb suggested it start with Spider-Man.

It is no surprise that a shy and scrawny nerdy kid from New York would say the hero we all needed wasn't some billionaire like Batman or muscled giant like the Hulk, but instead was an awkward, bullied nerd from New York who lived with his family and wanted nothing more than to fit in. The world needed Spider-Man more than ever.

The new Marvel president, seeing the opportunity to connect with a fresh and younger audience, brought in a team with the mission of revitalizing the wall-crawling hero. Soon after, they launched the *Ultimate Spider-Man* comic book, one of the best-selling series of all time. Within two years, this younger, more contemporary version of Spider-Man was played by Tobey Maguire at theaters across the world and earned an incredible $821 million at the global box office.

Over almost two decades, Gareb and his team not only brought people together, but entire industries, and as a result redefined the worlds of film, TV, gaming, pop culture, creative self-expression, and marketing. They set the stage for one of the largest and most active community cultures in the world. The only reason a geek like me had a chance to fit in growing up is because Gareb Shamus created a place where I was welcome. Now cosplayers, collectors, super fans, geeks, and nerds from every corner of comics, sci-fi, superheroes, and fantasy have a home. At conventions and online we see fans like Whovians (*Dr. Who*), True Believers (Marvel), Warsies (*Star Wars*), Gaters (*Stargate*), and Buffistas (*Buffy the Vampire Slayer*) hanging out with Bronies/Pegasisters (male/female fans of *My Little Pony*), Free Folk or Thronies (*Game of Thrones*), Schwifties (*Rick and Morty*), Trekkies (*Star Trek*), and countless other subcultures. They gather, dress up, talk about what they love, and have a place they call home. They are no longer isolated watching their shows, reading their stories, or playing their games, and for that, we owe Gareb and all the people he worked with a debt of gratitude.

Notice that Gareb didn't invent comic book fandom—the fans were there before he was even born. Instead, he gave them a place to come together and express themselves free of judgment. A place where the members of these subcultures could share an emotional connection. When you are a fan of comic books, shows, or story franchises, with that comes a mythology and history that you identify with. All *Star Wars* fans know about the Force, Darth Vader, and Luke Skywalker, any *Spider-Man* fan knows that Peter Parker regrets deeply not stopping the criminal who killed Uncle Ben, and that with great power comes great responsibility. And, of course, every Harry Potter fan knows of Lord Voldemort. *Wizard* magazine and, in time, Gareb's Comic-Cons gave all these fans a place to connect around a history and mythology they loved.

Remember, when Marvel was on the decline, it was a rebooted Spider-Man that gave young comic book fans a chance to participate in a shared history and mythology. Then when it came to box offices, even more people were welcomed in. Now with all the Marvel movie blockbusters, you would be hard pressed to meet a child or adult who doesn't know the story of the Avengers.

It doesn't matter if your community is religious and shares a spiritual history, political and shares a historical challenge, or fantasy and shares a wondrous and playful mythology, it all serves to connect those who identify with it. Whether your community shares a real or invented history isn't important—what is important is that you have something you can embrace and that brings you together. It could be that you read an article about walking and it inspired you to start a walking group, or that you and your friends think Julia Child was the greatest cook and you host a potluck to enjoy her recipes. Whatever it is, it is your shared journey.

Chances are there are people around the world and probably in your neighborhood who care about what you are interested in or would be if they knew about it. The beauty of community is that people are wired to find ways to connect. We just need to give them a place to come together. It could be as simple as meeting for breakfast at a coffee shop once a month, starting a group on Facebook or Reddit, or inviting some friends to play basketball.

Reading about what Gareb, Coss, and the Springboks accomplished may feel overwhelming. You may think *How do I do that?* For starters, what they accomplished happened over the course of decades, with small incremental improvements that added up to something incredible over time. But, more important, most of us don't have a desire to engage with millions of people like Gareb did. In most cases, an intimate community, company culture, or consistent get-together will be ideal. For those who are more introverted, small and personal bonding experiences are perfect. So, let's focus on what we want to do next, which is to bring together the people who are most important to you. Not only will it help you create, produce, and popularize whatever is important to you, but it will provide people a sense of community that will have unpredictably wonderful results for their lives.

When we began, I promised you that I would share a proven approach for developing real relationships with those you admire and respect, and that in the process not only would you accomplish what's important to you, but everyone's lives would improve. In Part

I, we discovered the incredible impact meaningful relationships have on our health, happiness, career, company, and causes. We also broke down what may be the most important equation in our lives, not because you will ever use it to calculate anything, but because the Influence Equation lets you understand how we can have an effect on our lives and the people we care about.

Influence = (Connection x Trust) $^{\text{Sense of Community}}$

You now know how to connect with anyone, build trust quickly, and develop a true sense of community. Frankly, this is where most books would end. They would say, *Now that you know these principles, go out there and apply them.* Unfortunately, understanding these principles and using them are two completely different things. Jean Nidetch knew that she needed to eat less to lose weight, but it wasn't until she had a structure supporting her that she could actually keep it off. Similarly, for us to succeed in creating meaningful connections, we need to learn how to apply these ideas.

Parts II and III are about understanding human behavior, with all of our wonderful irrationalities, and sharing the process for how to accomplish everything we have been talking about. So, prepare for fun stories, incredible science, and an approach you can use to bring the Influence Equation to life, because our next stop is the happiest place on earth.

Part II

The Path . . . Home

What to Do with the Influence Equation

Chapter 14

What Is a Path and How Will It Change Your Life?

———

As I work with people and organizations to cultivate relationships, one of the most common questions I get asked is: How will a guest respond to the event? They also might ask whether a particular person they want to meet will say yes to their invitation or want to connect with them. What they want me to do is use my experience and knowledge of behavioral science to predict a person's behavior. There is a certain comfort in being able to make these predictions, and if someone can learn to do that, they could always know the perfect approach for connecting with people. Google is a great example of how to predict behavior. In recent years, thanks to the massive quantities of data Google tracks on its users, it has seen incredible success predicting flu trends (accuracy as high as 97 percent), life spans of hospital patients (over 90 percent),[1] and, of course, what you are about to type. If any source has a chance of predicting a person's behavior, it would be Google. So, now I present you with an ethical question: When Google notices an uptick in violent searches, are they morally obligated to inform the police? Would it be negligent for them to ignore that?

If there was ever a person whose search history should have concerned authorities, it would be Jeff Davis. Initially, his searches were standard: directions and fun facts. But around 2004 they turned to murder, animal torture, ceremonial cult sacrifice, and serial killers. Year after year, these searches increased, but the authorities never showed up at his door to ask questions; as a result, as of February 2020, hundreds of innocent people are dead. Well, that's a bit misleading—

hundreds of innocent *characters* are dead. If you just looked at Jeff's Google search history, you would think he's a deranged killer. He is actually a wildly successful TV producer and writer, having created such hits as *Teen Wolf* and *Criminal Minds*.

Jeff is nothing like his searches. He is supportive, known for giving actors their first break and for hosting communal workouts with his writing team. So why is it that our predictions about Jeff and the reality are so poorly lined up? The answer lies in Jeff's show.

Although *Criminal Minds* is a fictional drama, it is based on the FBI's National Center for the Analysis of Violent Crime. There are several behavioral analysis units (BAUs) in this organization. Over an incredible 15 seasons and 324 episodes, the show follows a BAU of professionally trained criminal profilers as they attempt to stop serial killers. In an average episode, someone is killed, and the BAU is called in to figure out who the "unsub" (unknown subject of the investigation) is, and how to catch them before they strike again. To do this, the real BAU agents rely on years of experience, training, and taking critical insights from crime scenes to describe who the suspect is and where to find them.

On shows like *Criminal Minds*, *Profiler*, and *Mindhunter*, we get to see the awe-inspiring levels of insight these professionals have. It makes for very compelling television, especially when combined with kidnapped victims, chase scenes, computer graphics, and lives hanging in the balance. So, what can the world's best profiles teach us about predicting a person's behavior? Unfortunately, almost nothing.

Jeff would be the first to tell you, although criminalists have come a long way in understanding the patterns of serial killers, behavioral analysis units are absolutely awful at profiling people. They really can't predict much of anything. According to Davis, "It's pretty well known that the behavioral analysis unit doesn't actually catch killers, they just help narrow an investigation. Sometimes the profiles can be astonishingly accurate, sometimes astonishingly wrong. Of course, it makes for better TV when they're accurate. We want our TV detectives to make incredible leaps of deduction, but reality can be much more banal. After all, it was a parking ticket that finally led to the arrest of David Berkowitz, the Son of Sam."

In most industries, we expect experts to significantly outperform novices. If I played basketball almost as well as a first-round draft pick for the NBA, there would be a problem. But in a meta-study (when researchers review large collections of studies on a topic and find the patterns), researchers discovered that profiler/experienced-investigator groups were only "marginally better at predicting overall offender characteristics" than comparison groups, and were no better at predicting offenders' social habits, history, physical characteristics, and thinking.[2] This is concerning—if profiling is a professional, learnable skill, they should be significantly better than the public at identifying criminals.

What Jeff and criminal profilers teach us is that even with years of training and experience, it is near impossible to predict a single person. It is tempting to think that if we just had the right approach, we could connect with a specific person, but any one person is far too unpredictable. The reason that Google does such a good job with its predictions or even giving you search results is that they look at what billions of people are searching for and can see exceptionally large trends. It means that most of the time it will give you what you are looking for, but not always. It also means that when one person searches for the flu it is meaningless—they could be mistyping "flute," researching a TV show, or confirming they don't have it. When a million people search for the flu, we begin to see a trend, and these trends may be telling us something. This is why it didn't matter that Jeff was searching for how to kill someone. For the time being, a single person's behavior is far too unpredictable for us to focus on. That may change one day, but for now, our best bet is to look at how large numbers of people behave and understand that some of the individual people we interact with won't act consistently.

In the early days of creating the Influencers I was really interested in hosting specific people I admired or wanted to meet. I would try to predict exactly what to say or what they cared about, but I had to accept that it wouldn't work. Instead of focusing on one person, I needed to focus on people. I needed to create a sense of community. The fact is, there will always be someone we will want to know who won't be interested, and most of the time the reason has nothing to do with us. Instead of obsessing about the outliers, our job is to pay attention to the community as a whole. It is not important that any one person is part of it, but that the type of people we care about are part of it. Instead of trying to predict a person's behavior, let's learn from Google and look at how large numbers of people behave. While Google does an incredible job understanding behavior online, we want to learn from those who are the best at doing this in person. Clearly, they aren't profilers, so who are they?

In my opinion, they are theme park designers. Because these parks have millions of visitors and the environment is completely under control, any time they make a change, they can see the effect of it. If complaints increase, sales go up, or the amount of time guests spend at the park changes, they can take that information and tweak the design.

If you have ever been to Walt Disney World in Orlando, Florida, you may have noticed a certain design quirk. After parking, standing in line, and buying your entrance ticket, you can't directly enter the park. In fact, you and the other park attendees must enjoy either a boat ride or a monorail to get to the main entrance of the Magic Kingdom. After about twenty-three minutes from when you boarded, you and your fellow riders finally reach the front gate and the iconic sight of Disney's Main Street as children run toward Cinderella Castle.

Now the question: If Disney's goal is to be the happiest place on earth and run a successful, highly profitable business, why would the ticket counter be twenty-three minutes away from the main entrance? You could have been enjoying yourself and spent money in that time. Unexpectedly, the answer may have a lot to do with people's income.

Let's put it in perspective. In 2019 the average household income in the United States after taxes was between $32,000 and $59,000,[3] so let's split the difference at about $45,000. This means the average family has about $3,800 every month to pay for food, rent, clothing, health care, cell phone bills, car payments, credit card bills, and so on. Unfortunately, that means half of Americans earn much less than that. So, when mom or dad pay $1,200 for a four-day Disney pass for the family, that is a big deal to them, and that money doesn't include food, toys, hotel, or travel. In the moment they pass their credit card to the person at the counter, it all hits them. It's like spending their mortgage and car payment at once, and suddenly they experience the all too familiar frustration and regret of buyer's remorse. But if Walt Disney World is supposed to be the happiest place on earth, how do they deal with this?

The answer has become a bit of theme park mythology. Disney looked at the data, and although the buyer's remorse lasts different lengths of time depending on the person—how much they spent and how much they earn—that twenty-three-minute ride is long enough for you and your fellow riders to get over it. This means if you buy a ticket and board the monorail, by the time you get to the front gates of the Magic Kingdom, you will have either forgotten about the expense or at least feel more at ease about it, and will be excited to enjoy the happiest place on earth (and, of course, spend more money).

Some theme park experts suggest this was just a happy side effect of the layout of the park, but if it was intentional, I consider this one of the most brilliant examples of human-focused design I have ever seen. Disney realized their end goal: to make sure you enjoy every moment of your experience and to run a successful business. If you or the other park visitors walk in angry and annoyed from buyer's remorse, that's only going to lead to a bad experience, and you'll regret spending the money and won't want to come back. Instead, guest behavior is taken into consideration during design phases so that everyone has a better experience. Families are happier, they create better memories, the mood in the park is better, and as a result the business does better.

I love this example for two reasons: the first is that it perfectly demonstrates what behavioral economist Dan Ariely calls being "predictably irrational." The way we make decisions and react often don't make any sense, but they consistently don't make sense in the same way every time. Just look at how people make the same New Year's resolution year after year, and they really think this year it's going to be different. It is irrational to believe anything has changed, and predictable that people will keep doing it. The second is that when we learn how these irrational behavioral mechanics work, we can design around them. At Walt Disney World, even though everyone knows the ticket price ahead of time and is only standing in line because they agreed to it, the moment the purchase is made, our mechanics kick in and many people feel buyer's remorse. We aren't being forced to buy the tickets—we opted in, and yet we still feel bad. Unfortunately, buyer's remorse is part of our behavioral mechanics. It is a by-product of a bias known as loss aversion. In essence, we feel more pain from losing something than the pleasure of gaining it. For most people losing $100 hurts twice as much as the joy of gaining $100. Clearly, that isn't rational thinking, and the feelings should be equal. There is very little our rational minds can do when the mechanics and biases are running. And this leads us to an important nuance. Disney didn't try to guess or predict how people behave like a profiler would; instead they looked at how people actually act, and they designed around human behavior so that the experience would be exceptional.

When we design around human behavior, we can create a situation in which everyone is better off. This should be our goal when connecting with people: we need to let go of how we think people should behave and look at what people actually do. Once we are aware of people's mechanics, biases, and habits, we can design around them the way that Disney did and create opportunities so that people are most open to connecting, building trust, and creating a sense of community.

After learning about the Disney example, I changed the way people were welcomed to our events. Although we have never charged,

I added some transition time so they could unwind. Instead of just giving people a cocktail as they entered and leaving them with a group of strangers, we wanted to reduce the pressure of conversation. So, we started doing tours of people's homes or their art and assigning people jobs like bartender or coat person. We could see these little changes reduced stress and increased chatter.

When we understand the effects of our mechanics, we can plan around them, allowing us to be more considerate of people and what they need to feel like they belong.

The problem we face is that loss aversion, along with the IKEA effect, halo effect, and implicit egotism, are just a handful of a growing list of over 180 known cognitive biases that affect everything from whom we marry to what we buy, how we vote in an election, and what we notice and even what we don't notice. By learning about our mechanics, we can not only understand how to better connect with people but also to occasionally make a better decision or two. For example, a bias known as the decoy effect can have a beautifully irrational effect on our choices. I chose this one simply because it easily demonstrates how irrational we are. Sellers found that when customers select between two options, adding a third irrelevant option—a decoy—they are more likely to buy the high-priced item of the original two.

The classic example comes from the annual subscription pricing of the *Economist* magazine. Participants were split into two scenarios—the first with a decoy, the second without. On the next page are the subscription scenarios and the percent of people who chose each option.

Clearly, in scenario 1 no rational person would pick the decoy option of print alone for $125, when you could get print & online for the same price. But in scenario 2, when we remove the option no one wanted, we see far fewer people pick the more expensive choice of print & online. Instead, twice as many people now chose the less expensive option of online only.[4] To put this in perspective, adding a decoy is equivalent to telling a waiter you want to switch your dinner from chicken to beef because there is now a third option for a three-day-old cheese sandwich from the trash.

Subscription Scenario 1	
Option and Price	Selection Percentage
Online: $59	16%
Print: $125	0%
Print & Online $125	84%

Subscription Scenario 2	
Option and Price	Selection Percentage
Online: $59	32%
Print & Online: $125	68%

It is important to understand that we are all affected by these biases. Even you. In fact, thinking that others are affected more is called a bias blind spot and is another example of these well-documented behavioral quirks. At a certain point we have to accept that these are built-in limitations of the brain. It is tempting to think that if we could use more of our brains somehow, maybe go beyond that 10 percent limit everyone talks about, we would make better decisions. Neuroscientist Moran Cerf points out that the problem with this theory is that we already use 100 percent of our brains. He believes the misinformation comes as a result of our conscious minds being very limited in what they can control (e.g., we can't control whether we see the world in black and white or color or feel warm when it is cold out).

Cerf compares the brain to a piano. When pianists perform, they only use a few of the keys at a time; if they were to hit all of them simultaneously, it would both sound terrible and be a waste of a lot of energy. Similarly, the brain activates the specific areas that it needs when it needs them; there is no point in activating all of it at once. In fact, too much activity could result in devastating effects like seizures.

Ultimately, our brains want to use as little energy as possible, so we don't constantly need to find more food to fuel them. Thinking is very energy consuming. This is the reason we have cognitive biases—they function as shortcuts so we can make decisions quickly without using a lot of energy. If you were to go through a thorough detailed review of every possible factor each time you made a decision, you would go crazy. Picking out an ice cream cone would involve reviewing the supplier list for each of the ingredients, the ethical implications of eating something imported vs domestic, and the carbon impact, not to mention the wages of the employees, their company policies, and countless other factors just to get a scoop of chocolate ice cream. It makes no sense for us to use this much energy and time for a few sugary and tasty calories. Instead, we need a shortcut like this ice cream is organic, it is locally sourced, or it is made by a brand with a fun logo, so I will get a scoop.

Similarly, our brain developed over the course of millions of years and has tons of these shortcuts built into it, so we don't have to think about every aspect of every decision all the time. Brains are so hardwired that not only do we not notice these shortcuts, but we justify and explain them away. I will emphasize this again because it is a very important point. Our conscious mind has a habit of giving a really great narrative explanation for our biases. You may choose print & online because of a decoy effect, but when asked you will say you picked it because it was what you really wanted.

This is a brilliant solution for survival. Instead of having to worry about eating constantly, let's create shortcuts that work in most situations in order to reduce our effort to hunt and gather and increase our chances of survival. Regardless of what the choice was, let our conscious minds give a great narrative or explanation so we feel comfortable with our actions. Don't get me wrong—at times they work against us, we experience buyer's remorse or eat a more expensive meal because of a decoy, but chances are, if we didn't develop these biases, our ancestors never would have had the resources to feed a constantly running brain and we would have gone extinct.

The funny thing about these biases is that even when we are aware of them, we are still affected by them. It's like knowing you shouldn't date someone who is bad for you doesn't stop you from being attracted to them. Likewise, knowing that you will experience buyer's remorse doesn't stop you from feeling it after buying something. Instead, understanding the process means that we can do two things. As individuals we can take a step back and think: "Is this the choice or behavior that actually makes sense for me and what I care about?" This isn't something we can do all the time, as it can be exhausting, but it is an important practice. The second thing we can do is design around these biases, like Disney did with the entrance to Walt Disney World.

Now we have a strategy: rather than try to predict people, we can look at how our mechanics work and design around them. By taking into account all the amazing irrationality of human decision making, we can create better connections, greater levels of trust, more influence, and stronger communities. To accomplish this, we need to become behavioral architects or designers. The way theme park designers take people's behavior into account when they architect the environment, so will we.

Imagine for a moment that the human brain is like an elephant with a rider. The analogy is not perfect, but just go with me on this one. The rider is our conscious brain—it can speak and direct our actions. The elephant is our unconscious brain, which includes emotions, biases, and automatic systems. The rider is nowhere near as strong as the elephant, but when the rider has a lot of energy it can guide the elephant where it needs to go.

For example, in the morning when I wake up, I'm really great about eating healthy. Throughout the day I get progressively more tired, and as I do, my rider wears out. By the evening, my rider doesn't have the energy to control my elephant, so when my elephant sees a chocolate bar on my kitchen counter, it will eat every ounce of it. My conscious mind/rider has two options:

1. Get really mad at myself for not following through on my diet.

2. Justify the behavior with second-rate logic knowing the elephant will have his way.

This is where I believe my conscious mind shines. I am a really creative person, but nowhere in my life have I come close to the level of creativity I have used to justify eating a chocolate bar, going to meet friends for a drink, or anything else my elephant has wanted to do.

To overcome these types of problems, people have tried to convince the rider to behave better and be stronger. They help people build up their willpower and self-confidence. This is a very noble effort and can have a huge impact on people's lives. The next option is to appeal to the elephant. You want your dad to lose weight? Cry uncontrollably in front of him, telling him that you are worried that he will die and never make it to your wedding. Done right, you may be able to appeal to the elephant. But appeals to the elephant or rider won't work without a third option.

Regardless of where the elephant and the rider are going and who is in control, they have to walk down a path. If that path is very wide, the elephant can wander and cause trouble. On the other hand, if that path is designed well, the elephant has no choice but to go where we want it to go.

Your elephant can want all the chocolate in the world, but if you have none in the house and all the stores are closed, it's not going to get any. This is a very simple path design, but you can see it works. Our goal is to architect our experiences to take people down a path that ideally appeals to both the rider's logic and the elephant's emotions, biases, and mechanics, but ultimately gets them where they need to end up.

This is the beauty of what Walt Disney World accomplishes on their monorail/boat ride. You have a beautiful and novel experience that will take you to the front gate, and in that time everyone's elephants get over buyer's remorse, and not only does Disney physically get you where you want to go, but they got you where you emotionally wanted to be. Notice Disney didn't try to predict where you will be emotionally and meet you there; instead they designed a path that takes into account most people's elephant and rider. This means you can walk in remorseful, excited, sad, or even angry, and by the end of the ride you will be happier and ready to enjoy the park and create great memories.

Now we need to understand how we can design a path to make our experiences connecting with people just as effective and enjoyable. As you learn the design process, you will be able to apply it to anything from having people recognize the importance of your social cause so they support it to the value of the product you are marketing so they buy it to the impressive skills you have so you get hired. Now it's time to see how a legendary coach used this approach to cultivate one of the most successful teams in athletics history.

Chapter 15

Designing a Path

———

When Valorie Kondos was offered the position of head coach for the UCLA women's gymnastics team, she was a little surprised. She knew nothing about gymnastics, but having been a professional ballerina did give her some background in movement and choreography. What Valorie lacked in coaching experience she made up for with her ability to perform. She realized that all she needed to do was learn what the best and toughest coaches in history did, and then perform like them. She modeled coaches who were relentless dictators, so when athletes weren't behaving, she would yell at them. Thanks to her great performance skills, the results were immediate. They went from a respected gymnastics program when she took over to one of the worst in the country in under two years.

Valorie was more than a little lost. As she walked into the UCLA sports complex, she paused and stared at the building. Every year, the school spent around $50 million to train student athletes. She had been hired to do two things: win and get her student athletes to graduate. She struggled with the absurdity of spending so much money on bragging rights. In all honesty, it wasn't a culture she cared about. As a professional dancer, all she cared about was enjoying the process and growing from it. But as she sat in her office that day, she came to terms with something. She wasn't tough talking, relentless, or hard as nails. In fact, she is one of the most compassionate and caring people you could ever meet. She was hired to win, but truth be told that wasn't what she was hungry for. She wanted to improve her athletes' lives; she wanted to develop whole human beings.

UCLA is a magnet for recruiting; after all, sunny California and the culture of Los Angeles sound great to a seventeen-year-old who is venturing on their own for the first time. This meant that Valorie had the privilege of coaching some of the most elite gymnasts in the world; many of them had already competed in the Olympics by the time they reached her. Because of the incredible risk of injury and the authoritarian coaching style the sport is known for, these athletes tend to be exceptionally good at following instructions. So, Valorie realized her goal shouldn't be to push these young women harder—they had been yelled at and controlled their entire lives. She tried that for years and not only did it not work, but it made her and them miserable. So success for her "shifted from only focusing on winning to developing my coaching philosophy, which is developing champions in life through sport."[1] This meant she would bring her whole heart to her student athletes and help them develop into extraordinary people. Since things couldn't get much worse from a ranking perspective, if they failed, at least their lives would improve along the way.

As Valorie set a new standard for herself and goal for the team, she didn't need to perform anymore. Instead, she could be her loving, fun, wholehearted self. Her coaching turned from the sport to life. She talked to the girls about making good decisions and healthy living. Calls with young recruits focused almost entirely on them and what they cared about and had almost nothing to do with training. As her student athletes became more empowered, they trusted her more and performed better. Over the next twenty-five years, the UCLA Bruins women's gymnastics team won seven NCAA championships and Miss Val, as her athletes called her, was inducted into the UCLA Athletic Hall of Fame and voted Pac-12 Coach of the Century. Although this is a testament to her incredible success, if this was all she had accomplished, she would have considered herself a failure. For her, "Real success is developing champions in life, win or lose."[2] Success was helping these young women become great people.

Several years in, Miss Val's values were put to the test. One of her student athletes, Kyla Ross, came into her office and in what was completely uncharacteristic of her, sat down on the couch and started talking to Miss Val about her classes and future aspirations. By this point, Miss Val had earned Kyla's trust, and as they continued to chat, it was clear that this wasn't going to be a normal conversation. For the first time in her life, Kyla shared that she had been sexually abused by the former USA Gymnastics team doctor Larry Nassar. Soon after, Kyla came forward with the other victims, taking a brave stand and preventing Nassar from hurting others. As a result, Nassar was later convicted for being a serial sex offender.

As she sat in her office after Kyla's revelation, Valorie had two options: she could either focus the team completely on their forthcoming NCAA championship and avoid what could potentially be an explosive distraction that could trigger other victims or their friends, or she could address it straight on and use it as an opportunity to help develop champions in life. Valorie was clear about what her responsibility was; winning the championship at the cost of her athletes' emotional well-being was not acceptable. Over the next weeks she dedicated several team meetings to addressing the issue, creating a safe space for Kyla and the team to work through it. Kyla was fortunate to have a coach and team that could support her. It is impossible to imagine the trauma and pain the 250-plus victims Nassar abused experienced and still live with. Thankfully, there were those who were able to come forward so that he is not still practicing medicine or hurting innocent children.

Later that year, UCLA won the Women's Gymnastics National Championship. Afterward, Kyla told Miss Val that she felt one reason they'd won was because Val had addressed the issue. Kyla said, "Miss Val, I literally felt myself walk taller as the season went on, and when I walked onto that championship floor, I felt invincible."

Ultimately, this was Valorie's point: winning at the cost of dignity, humanity, and joy is an empty win. She made it her personal responsibility to help the girls develop their whole selves by harnessing the strength needed not only to win in competition but also to grow into extraordinary women of character. She believed that developing champions in life would translate to success in competition, and clearly this worked. In interviewing Miss Val for this book, it was clear that she embodies many of the lessons we covered, from building trust and being benevolent to developing a true sense of community, but what she is truly masterful at is understanding how to create an effective path for the elephant and the rider. She knew exactly where she wanted her student athletes to end up on graduation day. It wasn't about technical skills—they already had those—but rather about character building so they could make great decisions with or without a coach present. Compared to her previous goal of being tough as nails, this was a path she and her coaching team were inspired to design and would share with their athletes while continuing to instill critical core values and lessons through team meetings, one-on-one conversations, practices, and exercises. They created a development journey that empowered the students so that when they accepted their diploma, they would be ready to live their own lives confidently.

When creating a path, most people, companies, and organizations develop a simple three-stage process to get your attention, interact with you, and hopefully gain your membership. This could be recruiting for UCLA gymnastics or becoming a customer of a subscription service. I describe these stages as:

1. *Discovery:* How to get your attention (an ad, an invitation, an introduction, etc.), that will lead you to . . .

2. *Engagement:* You connect with the brand or person (buy the product, attend the event, meet in person, etc.), which will hopefully lead to . . .

3. *Membership:* You will continue to connect and consume (purchase more, participate in the next events, maintain a friendship, etc.).

This is a lovely idea, and it sounds very reasonable, but it has one big flaw in it: it is designed backward. When you plan a journey, you don't begin by looking where you are and just walking or driving to your destination; instead you look at where you want to end up and plan back from there.

As a child, when I wanted to figure out the fastest way through a maze, I would start at the end and work my way back to the beginning. Similarly, Val's success came when she picked a destination that inspired her, and then she worked her way back from graduation day to design the path. The process is the same for us; we want to look at the end result (in this case membership) and ask what kind of membership we want to create. How do you want people to interact with you and feel when they do? For Val, membership was about having her student athletes on a journey of growth together. That feels and looks very different from the traditional image of an authoritarian-run gymnastics team. For Val to create her ideal membership, she would need to look at ways she could engage her student athletes that would produce that sense of membership and comradery. Only once we are clear about how we want to engage with people should we consider how we approach them. Notice that once Val was clear on the type of membership she wanted, she changed the way that training was done (Engagement) and then the way she approached new recruits (Discovery). If she would have tried to do it the other way—by starting with designing the recruiting process—then recruiting wouldn't have lined up with engagement and neither would align with the membership she needed. It would be the equivalent of getting in the car for a drive and hoping you end up at a destination you like. You want to define what you stand for and make sure your message is clear before you start advertising it or inviting people to join. By starting with membership, you can create the kind of culture and values you want to focus on.

Not all membership is the same. Red Bull managed to get people to launch themselves off piers; meanwhile Apple has people sleeping out overnight to be among the first for a new phone they could have just ordered online. Some people will give you a kidney, others won't give you the time of day, so when you think about your community, ask yourself what kind of membership you want to have with your customers, donors, supporters, friends, community members, employees, and so on. And here is the most important part: it has to be consistent with your values and the brand's values. There is no way you will be able to develop a real connection with people year after year, event after event, product release after release if you are not inspired by and committed to those values. You will hate it.

This was Miss Val's turning point when she entered the UCLA training facility. She realized that the values she assumed were needed to win had to be "at all costs." Not only was this something she didn't believe in, but it was diametrically opposed to her values of loving, caring for, and helping people develop. Once she accepted that, she could create a new goal that was consistent with her values: developing champions who brought confidence and health into their lives beyond the competition floor. Now it was obvious that this wouldn't be possible if she continued to engage with her student athletes as a dictator. This meant she had to redesign her entire engagement process. It meant rewriting team meetings, talking about personal development, and creating a profound level of trust. In time she grew as a coach, and the team grew in success. When she focused on teaching the team to make effective decisions, they would take better care of themselves, they wouldn't go out partying before a competition, and they wouldn't put up with abuse from their boyfriends.

Once we know what kind of membership we want to create, we can design how we engage people to produce it. We want to create a pathway or a process for the right people to opt in and those who don't fit the culture to self-select out. For example, cutthroat athletes who lash out at team members probably don't belong in Miss Val's program.

As far as the discovery processes for Miss Val's program, that was the easy part for her. It is commonplace for a coach to call or meet with potential recruits and their families. Her discovery calls focused on the person with a goal of developing champions in life, and those same values ran through all the way to membership.

Although we live life going forward, when it comes to developing profound results, influence, community, and so on, we have to design backward. Val started with the end in mind then built the program backward from there, and that is what we will do.

Membership: What do we want people to feel, think, and do?
Engagement: What will lead to this type of membership?
Discovery: What attracts the right people to engage in this way?

Val's path was brilliant. Not only did she address each of the above stages, but she appealed to the rider by talking about making good decisions and building mental fortitude. She also appealed to the elephant by creating a strong emotional bond with her student athletes. The path had structure to make sure the elephant couldn't wander too much. She had a clear training process, assistant coaches, trainers, and supporters who made sure these athletes wouldn't lose their way.

When we are working on creating connection, we don't have the luxury of training people over the course of years. We maybe have seconds with them over email, minutes over a phone call, or a couple of hours if it is an intimate in-person event. This means that the path we design needs to be much more planned out. So now you might be thinking, *How do I design my path and what do I need to focus on in the process?* I'll give you an example from my own experience. It took place several years after I started the community, so it isn't about starting a group but rather focuses on how my team and I design an event for maximum impact.

On Saturday, March 7, 2015, a group of sixty of my dinner alumni received their final confirmations to the Aesthetic Scentability Brunch. They were instructed:

- Brunch will be provided (no need to cook for me this time)
- Bring the names and addresses of three loved ones
- A world expert will be flown in to teach you something

They were also told that this event was partnered with a company and they should be prepared for a fun surprise.

Guests entered to a delicious brunch buffet, cocktails, and even some games for them to connect over. After some food, the surprise: twelve people at a time were pulled into a separate room, and two at a time were assigned to tables covered in flowers and were greeted by one of the most respected professional florists around.

Over the next thirty minutes, the florist demonstrated the theory and technique of assembling the perfect bouquet while guiding the group to make their own. Once they were done with their bouquets, each of the guests revealed who they were. A petite woman in the front was famed sexologist Dr. Ruth Westheimer; next to her was Tom DeSanto, producer of *X-Men* and *Transformers*; then the editor-in-chief of *Elle* at the time, Robbie Myers; and the list continued to other celebrities, journalists, authors, and professional athletes, until the last person said: "My name is Ajay Kori, I'm the founder of UrbanStems. We deliver beautiful bouquets anywhere in the city at a modest price. We wanted to thank you for coming, so we have delivery people waiting who will deliver your bouquets to your loved ones right now." While people were mingling and having fun, they would be sent a photo of their loved ones receiving their bouquets.

You might think that sounds like a lot of fun, but there is a lot going on here. Let's break down why we designed the experience the way we did so we can understand how this relates to the path we want the elephant and the rider to walk down.

Membership

Let's start with the end. What kind of membership do we care about, how do we want people to feel, and what are the core values of the brand?

For UrbanStems, flower delivery is about the joy of making other people feel special. When someone thinks "show appreciation," we want them to associate the desire to do so with an UrbanStems arrangement.

To instill this feeling, we designed around a cognitive bias known as the peak-end rule, which has to do with the way people process experiences. Imagine you are on the best date of your life. Three hours in, as you are leaning in for a kiss, your date looks you in the eyes and says . . . the most awful thing you have ever heard. As soon as you get home your friend asks: "Good date or bad date?" What do you say?

Even though it was three hours of perfection followed by only three seconds of awfulness, everyone says it was awful. According to research by Nobel laureate Daniel Kahneman, human beings can't process the duration of pleasure or pain—what they remember disproportionally are the peaks of an experience and how they end.

Employing the peak-end rule meant we wanted to end on the emotional values of the brand, and we accomplished that by surprising people with photos of their loved ones receiving the bouquets they had just assembled. This would be the trigger for the membership.

Engagement

Once we were clear on the intended end result, we planned out how we would engage people. Rather than give you every detail, I will share the broad strokes of our thinking.

The company wanted to connect with industry influencers, so

we were building around generosity, novelty, curation, and awe. We weren't concerned about generosity and curation because we were providing a free event, but it still left us with novelty and awe. We needed something like a presentation, game, or activity. We considered many options, but we also wanted to build trust and a greater connection to the brand, so we leaned on the IKEA effect. Having the guests assemble bouquets while they learned about the flowers would make them value UrbanStems more, but it wouldn't blow their mind or trigger awe. After a lot of brainstorming, we came up with the gift of flower delivery and photos of their loved ones receiving the bouquets; we knew it would give them goose bumps. We hoped that combining that experience with discovering who their fellow guests were would trigger awe. Even if we didn't, the exercise of setting a goal of creating an awe-inspiring moment enabled us to develop a better concept.

Discovery

In this example, we were inviting mostly people who had been to one of my events before, so there was a base level of trust. But we still made sure our communication had multiple points to appeal to people.

The first was that we included hints or explicitly mentioned the basic characteristics of generosity, novelty, and curation (we'll leave out awe since we can't guarantee it). Second, we made it mysterious. Since the entire floral experience was a surprise, we hinted at what would happen and cultivated curiosity. This is a behavioral mechanism known as information gaps. When there is a gap between what we know and what we are presented with, one of three things happens. If the gap is too big (e.g., someone at a party talks to us about something we have no understanding of, like theoretical particle physics), we are uninterested and want to leave the situation. If the gap is too small (e.g., someone lets you know the date), it doesn't raise any questions because it isn't a surprise. But if the gap is in that sweet spot where it is not so large that you want to avoid it and not so small that it is uninteresting, you become curious.

For examples, look at the title of any *BuzzFeed* article. The interesting characteristic of curiosity is that it feels like an itch you can scratch. Your brain feels a necessity to engage in order to get an answer. So, when *BuzzFeed* publishes an article like "27 Uses for a Banana, Number 15 Will Blow Your Mind," you can't help but click it. Unfortunately, number 15 has never blown my mind. Instead of producing clickbait like *BuzzFeed* does, we created curiosity about the event and then delivered something satisfying so guests are happy they engaged.

We named it the Aesthetic Scentability Brunch. The name doesn't make any sense, so you read it over and over again wondering, should it say "sensibility"? What does scent have to do with it? Then we increase the curiosity when we tell them that a world expert will be there to teach them something. They wonder who the expert will be, what new skills they will learn, and even who the other guests are. If you use this approach for creating curiosity, then the answer needs to be satisfying; it can't be clickbait. Once you see the flowers and learn how to assemble them, you realize it is aesthetic and you can smell it, so it is scentable. It may not be a real word, but the conclusion is satisfying.

Now you can see that the discovery process is built to lead them to that specific engagement and in turn to the specific type of membership and feeling. We appeal to the elephant and the rider and we designed an effective path to get us where we want to go.

According to my client at UrbanStems, at the time this was the most effective event they had ever done, especially considering its modest budget. Most PR firms or event teams would have focused on inviting a bunch of Instagrammers/socialites to a party hoping they would post about it. Don't get me wrong, that type of event can have value, but it doesn't create a strong emotional connection to the brand. It doesn't establish a meaningful relationship to the leadership of the company. Instead, using this approach after the event, Ajay could have sent an email to almost anyone in the group and they would have been responsive. This approach led to new customers, potential celebrity partnerships, and a significant number of media stories. Most important, instead of renting those relationships from a PR firm, those relationships belonged and stayed with Ajay and his team for years to come.

With so many cognitive biases and behavioral quirks in existence, it can be hard to know which ones to focus on. In the early stages, I would recommend the three we covered in the Aesthetic Scentability Brunch. During discovery, focus on creating curiosity by using information gaps so guests will be enticed to connect. You could also use loss aversion during discovery by reminding people how disappointed they would be if they missed it, sometimes called FOMO (fear of missing out), or you can use scarcity by limiting the number of open spots and letting them know that it will fill up soon, so they should act fast. But remember two important criteria. The first should be obvious: do not lie to people; it will ruin your reputation. The second is that if you create curiosity or loss aversion, you have to make sure the experience of attending is worth it or people will feel tricked like they do from a bad clickbait article.

When engaging, build around the IKEA effect so participants will invest group effort. This will have them bond more to each other and you or your brand. To instill the membership values, try to apply the peak-end rule so people develop a strong emotional connection and remember it. Over time this will lead to a greater sense of community. I want to emphasize again the importance of designing around human behavior in an ethical way. The simple test is: If I share with participants every behavior I designed around and why, would they be okay with it? I sleep easy because I regularly break down the science at the end of a dinner, and people love it. Similarly, Val could tell her student athletes exactly why her program was designed the way it was, and those athletes would love her for it. If I ever used this knowledge for unbenevolent or dishonest reasons, I would quickly lose people's trust, and that would go against everything I built.

A CRITICAL REMINDER ON ETHICS

Something I will keep coming back to is that as we learn more about how biases work, we need to check in with ourselves and consider if we think we may be crossing some kind of moral or ethical boundary. As I've mentioned before, my general test is: If I shared with a participant, someone I wasn't friends with, every aspect of the design of the experience, would they feel manipulated or would they appreciate the thoughtfulness?

In Chapter 3, we discussed that trust is built on competence, honesty, and benevolence. This is a question of benevolence: Do you have the participant's or community member's best interests at heart?

If someone found out that the entire experience was designed to get participants addicted to cigarettes, they should be upset. It breaches benevolence. If the experience is designed for people to have fun and discover a brand or product that could be useful, there is no issue.

To prevent problems from occurring, we have two policies at Influencers that you may want to consider:

1.   Every time we have a brand involved with one of our events, it says so on the invitation.

2.   The brand shares its values, objectives, and budget, but we have full design control. We have always delivered for the brands but never at the expense of the community.

In this way we protect the community and ensure we always have their best interests in mind.

Putting this level of thought into a gathering may seem overwhelming, but don't be daunted. Over time, as you gather people, create an event, foster an online community, or even run a club, these considerations will start to evolve naturally. The first dinner I hosted was a mess. It was in the middle of the summer, my air conditioner broke, and the food was terrible. I cringe when I think about everything that went wrong. I had no money at the time, and I didn't have proper dinnerware to serve everyone. Looking back, it worked because of the flaws. It wasn't some glam party with superficial design; instead I was bringing people together for something novel and well curated. They saw the benevolence. In fact, having no clue what I was doing put me in a vulnerable state where people could pitch in and feel more connected. Whatever you create will be wonderful, and a little messy at the start, and that's how it should be. It gives your early community members a greater sense of ownership, and over time it will improve. You'll get to look back fondly and see how far you have come.

Now we have seen how to design a path for the elephant and the rider that takes people's behavior into account, entices them to connect, and cultivates trust. Next we want to understand how all of this works together to develop a sense of community and belonging that grows your influence and improves people's lives. For this, we will visit one of the largest creative communities in the world and learn how they went from an idea to a global phenomenon.

Chapter 16

Your Path for Creating Community

_____

When Tina Roth-Eisenberg came to the United States, she never expected leaving Switzerland would be so isolating. Her dream was to become a professional designer, and even though she managed to get an internship in a small design firm and make some friends, she hadn't yet met what she called "my people." She wanted to be part of a generous, open, inclusive creative community. Unfortunately, there were two challenges. The first was that, to put it politely, her English skills needed some improvement. It's hard to make friends when people don't understand you. The second was that all the creatives (designers, architects, filmmakers, etc.) that she wanted to connect with were siloed in their industries and didn't come together as a single community. To make matters worse, all the conferences and events were industry specific and expensive, which meant that people had to already be successful to afford the attendance fee. This exclusivity only served to further segment creative people.

As the years progressed, so did her command of the English language, and the popularity of Swiss Miss, her cleverly titled design blog. Her status as a popular blogger garnered her free passes to all the conferences she couldn't afford as a struggling intern, and this access only served to reinforce her belief that someone should bring these siloed communities together.

Tina decided to run an experiment. She would invite a group of creatives to her office to connect early one Friday morning. The event would be free, the coffee would be free, and the bagels would be free. It would be open to anyone. It wouldn't matter if you were a struggling college student who wanted to learn photography or a founder of a global architecture firm, you were welcome and you paid nothing. She called it CreativeMornings. She advertised it on her blog, and about sixty showed up early in the morning to a rundown building with a broken elevator. After the six-floor trek up the stairs, they were greeted with stale bagels and a promise that coffee would show up soon. But no one cared how bad the bagels were, because Tina bringing them together was enough of a reason to wake up early and meet before work.

The first event had no format, just mingling, but with each event she improved her design. In order to catalyze conversations between people, at the second event she added a talk by a designer and asked a local creative agency to host it. The twenty-minute talk and fifteen minutes of Q&A made it feel less like a networking event and more like a cultural moment. Simply put, it was less awkward, in particular for the introverts.

As the months went by, she continued to streamline the event. Smiling volunteers would greet guests and give them name tags with icebreakers on them. To inspire creativity and belonging the decor included handmade signs such as "You look great today," "Everyone is welcome," and "Everyone is creative." To foster connections, Tina created a collaboration station to pair people up based on career goals. As to ensure the content represented the values of the organization, in addition to talks by thought leaders, there were performances by musicians and even thirty-second pitches from attendees.

Since its inception in 2008, the CreativeMornings community has grown so much that Tina personally hosts over five hundred people every month, but she didn't stop there. She wasn't the only person looking to connect with "[her] people." She would get message after message from people around the world wanting to run Creative-Mornings in their local area. Tina, believing "trust breeds magic," opened it up to anyone who wanted to host and developed standard practices to ensure quality control. One of the rules was that sponsorships could be sold, but all the money would need to be invested in the events and community in order to ensure the spirit of the event was kept intact.

As of this book's writing, CreativeMornings runs free events for 25,000 people every month across 216 cities in 67 countries. Tina may have started as an isolated Swiss girl in a new country, but now she is a powerhouse leader with several successful startups surrounded with creatives who inspire her. Hundreds of thousands of people around the world have participated in CreativeMornings, and in the process developed relationships, married, started companies, learned new skills, and improved their careers, all because one day Tina decided to send an invite to a group of strangers.

As a designer, Tina created a path that brought the Influence Equation to life beautifully. She knew where that path needed to lead: to inspire creativity and connection. You will notice every aspect of discovery and engagement led to the type of membership she wanted, and each improvement she made strengthened it over time. Throughout the engagement process she continuously triggered cues for belonging and created opportunities for people to connect with one another, from name tags and greeters to the Collaboration Station. The path was so effective that even if a person came in grumpy from waking up early before work, they would be fed, caffeinated, inspired, and energized for days to come. She designed around where people are and where she wanted them to be.

All three parts of the Influence Equation were fulfilled. Tina's strategy to entice creatives to connect came from years of experience and instinct, but you will notice how it perfectly matches the SOAR model I described in Chapter 8. She provides people with skills, opportunities, access, and resources. Participating brings the members' creativity to life and gives them the insight, connections, and tools to accomplish what they care about.

Trust is cultivated from countless vulnerability loops, from volunteers offering their time to set up, film, and break down, to musicians and speakers contributing their talents, and even the act of being welcomed to the group and participating in an icebreaker or going to the Collaboration Station to be paired off with a fellow creative.

Every aspect of the experience comes together to give people a sense of community. Participants realize a clear boundary between the resignation of the outside world and the world of inspiration and belonging they get to participate in. It isn't a passive experience—members can give a talk or a pitch, volunteer, or create signs. They fundamentally have influence. Each time they participate, they grow their skills and their circle of creatives. They are all on the same journey, going in the same direction and sharing the same values of creativity and inspiration.

Surprisingly, Tina's greatest strength wasn't her design skills. In fact, it was something that required little to no skill: it was her consistency. It would be near impossible for people to feel a sense of community if they attended an event once and then never saw each other again. The types of relationships we are looking to create grow with time spent together, and especially through a consistent routine. Religious groups accomplish this through weekly events. Christians have Sunday church service; for Muslims Friday is called Al-Jumu'ah, which translates as "the day of congregation." This consistency offers a time for people to see one another, participate in rituals, and reinforce bonds. It is an opportunity for their sense of community to grow. And then there are offshoots such as prayer groups that meet throughout the week, volunteer opportunities, or group trips and tentpole events such as the high holidays that everyone can participate in.

Social groups have similar structures. Sports fans might go to the local bar every week to watch their team play; going in person would be an offshoot; and the final game of the season, when everyone watches even if their team isn't playing, would be the tentpole event. Similarly, the strength of CreativeMornings, Influencers, Weight Watchers, and ConBody workouts is the consistency of community gatherings. The following are the three basic categories; you only need to focus on the ones that suit what you are trying to accomplish.

- *Flagship:* This is the experience that is most consistent; it happens weekly, monthly, or on some other set cadence. For Influencers it is the Influencers Dinner; sports teams like the

Springboks have practices, while their fans have games; religions have service; and CreativeMornings have their morning events. For some organizations, this event is an initiation to the community or orientation at a company; for others it is the main platform.

- *Offshoot:* These are the secondary programs offered; they give subgroups an opportunity to come together around events, experiences, or topics they care about. At Influencers we do seven to ten custom events a year where we partner with outside companies like the Aesthetic Scentability Brunch (see page 152). Every month or two we host a Pride Workout for members of the LGBTQIA community and a Women of Influence event, and we have several others in the works for groups including people of color, nonprofits, and marketers. CreativeMornings has launched field trips in which members can host others in their offices to share what their company is like.
- *Large Gathering:* These are the big annual or seasonal events, sometimes known as tentpole events. American football has the Super Bowl, superhero fans have Comic-Con or the release of a long-awaited movie, and at the Influencers we have reunions and the Inspired Culture Salon series.

Depending on the size of the community you are looking to create or be a part of, in most cases all you need is a flagship event. CreativeMornings accomplishes its goal through a single event design that they run consistently around the world. At some point they chose to create field trips, which was a wonderful way to enable community members to get more involved without requiring Tina's time, but they would have done great with or without them. Considering their scale, they could run a large gathering once a year to bring together creatives from around the world, but since no money is taken from guests, they would either have to find a massive sponsor, develop an incredible volunteer program, or change the rules and charge people.

It's unclear if creating a large-format event would help them accomplish their goal any better than their current formats. As a general rule, avoid going big unless it really serves you. Scale involves more time, expense, and potential problems since they tend to be annual rather than weekly or monthly.

This is the structure I generally recommend. Once you develop a standard format, whether in person or online, run it several times, make sure to get the kinks out, and continuously improve it. This means creating an effective path and applying the Influence Equation. You won't get it perfect the first time, but you'll improve over time. If the standard format is already for fifty to one hundred or more, you may not need a larger gathering, but consider offshoot events. If you are hosting two to twenty or more at a time, and it is a changing group each time rather than a cohort (same people each time), your guests probably would like to meet each other. This is where the larger gatherings produce a sense of community. It is generally best to start small and build up. It's a less stressful and more enjoyable process, as massive events can be logistical nightmares and burn us out.

If we never invited people back after an Influencer's Dinner, guests might feel a connection to each other or to me but not a sense of community. So we developed Inspired Culture: The Salon by Influencers as a large gathering format so there is always an opportunity to invite people back and have them meet one another.

Consistency of events is critical. If people you want to host are busy this time, they'll know there is always the next one, or the one after that. It gives them a sense of stability, and communities that have structure and longevity demonstrate competence. Imagine you are in corporate sales and you have a novel gathering every week with friends and some potential customers. This gathering gives you a consistent reason to connect beyond just pitching your product. You can develop a relationship when they participate, and thanks to the consistency, when they have a need, you are top of mind. Creative-Mornings succeeded because of this consistent approach and improvement process.

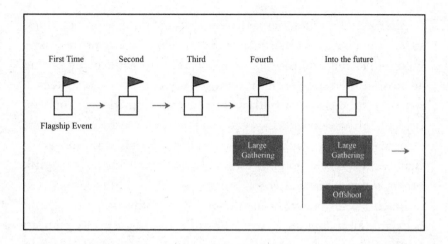

As the CreativeMornings community has grown over the past twelve years, Tina found her place where she and countless others could feel at home. With finding "[her] people" came incredible career opportunities. Tina now runs several successful companies, including a coworking space for creatives, a temporary tattoo company, a consultancy, and an ever-growing personal brand. Not only has she touched countless lives, but she has gained all the wonderful benefits of being a part of a community. Did it help that she was a designer? Sure, but remember, in the early days she was an immigrant with no money who barely spoke English. Her knowledge of design may have helped, but what led to her success more than anything else was her consistency. Since her first event with the stale bagels, she has run CreativeMornings every month for twelve years. She does this because she plays an infinite game. This may sound a little odd, so let me explain.

In 1986 James P. Carse published a wildly influential book titled *Finite and Infinite Games.* He suggested that in every aspect of life we play one of the two. Finite games have a beginning and end, you play to win, and there are agreed-upon rules (e.g., how long you play, what defines a win). Basketball is a finite game: after a set time, the game is over and the team with the most points wins. People can then play a new game if they want, but the first game is over—it is finite.

Alternatively, infinite games have no end and no agreed-upon rules, so you can't have a winner or a loser. People play them for the enjoyment of playing, and the objective is to keep the game going as long as possible. Marriage is an infinite game; you don't participate in a marriage to outscore or outlast your neighbors or friends. You participate for the value it brings you. And notice there are no universal rules of marriage—each couple plays differently. It is an infinite game that you try to keep going as long as possible. And when we pass on, others will be playing after.

Much like marriage, human connection, community, trust, and belonging all are infinite games. We play because of the joy we get from playing. The feeling of belonging is its own reward. Trying to win would be ridiculous because there is no way to win. Having a bigger community is not winning; you can be joyous living in a small, profoundly connected community that fits your values. Getting to play the game is reward enough. Although your influence will grow as you play, it is a by-product, not the goal.

As author Simon Sinek points out, when people or organizations play the wrong game, the results can be devastating. When Volkswagen faked its cars' emission results in order to make their products look better, or when Wells Fargo illegally opened bank accounts for customers, they may have had a short-term gain, but when their frauds came to light, both experienced incredible damage to their reputation. These companies are in the infinite game of business, but they were playing like it was finite. Their objective should have been to keep the game going as long as possible and to play for as long as they could. Instead executives got greedy and as long as they made their bonuses, they didn't care about the effects of their actions. Similarly, if we treat a community as a finite game, it turns from an experience of belonging into chess. Each person has a value, and they become pawns we use as means to an end. Eventually the trust and sense of community that we developed falls apart and we lose the very thing we worked so hard to create.

This is where Tina Roth-Eisenberg, Jean Nidetch, Coss Marte, and the other organizers profiled in this book have stood out: they played an infinite game. They've understood that by playing the game as a community, life improves and we accomplish what we care about, whether that's getting healthy, succeeding in business, promoting a cause, or even finding best friends. It may mean that some days you will meet and connect with incredible new clients, donors, or friends, and it will feel like you are winning. On other days, people won't be a good match, or your members won't be able to be in the community anymore because they move to another city, and it might feel like you are losing. This is when it's important to remember the game you are playing. It isn't about the numbers; it's about participating, connecting, and playing as long as we can. The game is a gift unto itself; it is in playing that the magic of life happens. Over the years that I have been playing, the following principles have helped me, and I hope they help you too.

It All Begins with Benevolence

If we don't have benevolent intentions, developing meaningful relationships and a sense of community will be nearly impossible. We may be able to connect with people in the short term, but over the long term, as our selfish intentions come to light, our reputations will be destroyed. All the social, career, and health benefits we gain from being connected will fall apart. I am not saying we need to be purely altruistic. It's fine for someone to sell me a product, but I want the salesperson to have my best interests at heart. And if I'm asked to support a cause, I want that nonprofit to understand how to respect my donation.

It's about Belonging and Feeling at Home

I hope you know the feeling of being excited to see old friends. The people you can say anything to and you aren't worried you will be judged. Unfortunately, this feeling of psychological safety is far too rare. When Google wanted to understand what makes teams effective, they ran a research program called Project Aristotle.[1] We generally imagine that the most effective teams, especially at a company like Google, are comprised of five to ten superstars from their respective areas of expertise. These superstars have a combined IQ of a billion and have won every award since they started talking at the age of three weeks. But what they found was surprising: the number one predictor of effective teams is what they called psychological safety. The teams that feel safe are willing to take risks and be vulnerable. As we learned, it is vulnerability loops that build trust and cause us to feel more connected. The teams that felt safe to say something that might be wrong or make a mistake outperformed those who had more thinking power. This does not mean that everyone should be a part of your community. Who the members are is up to you, but those who are on the inside should feel safe and have a sense of belonging.

Create a Platform and See the Community Grow

A person's sense of community comes from them; it isn't something someone else can give. Instead we can provide a platform where people can come together and have an experience that bonds them. Remember, your community is already out there; they just need a way to connect and congregate. You design a path so that people can find their way, and at the end of that path they experience a sense of belonging, of coming home and being with people who value what they value. This is the source of everyone being better off and the source of the influence you cultivate.

Provide an Initiation Experience

An initiation enables people to feel that they have overcome a rite of passage and are now members. As we saw with the sorority sisters, the more intense the initiation process, the more bonded people are to the group. Still, it is completely unnecessary to do anything painful (either socially or physically) like the bullet ants or teeth chiseling from Chapter 4. At CreativeMornings you are invited to stand up and be acknowledged before the talk or performance begins. This is a common experience that welcomes all participants. For the Influencers, simply coming to a dinner and cooking together is the initiation. Once someone has done that, they are on the "inside" and can come to any of our salons. They join our permanent invitation list and are always welcome.

Use an ABCD: Asset-Based Community Development Model

When a large company lacks a skill, they can hire someone, but in a community the option to find someone with a specific expertise and having them fit in is much more complex. Instead, strong communities tend to follow an asset-based community development (ABCD) model. Instead of focusing on the things they lack, ABCD suggests growing from the skills and resources their members already have. This approach enables members to contribute and be proud of what they produce. This is also true for developing a stronger company culture; using an ABCD approach will create a greater sense of contribution and connection.

I want to point out that connecting with people may be an infinite game, but that doesn't mean you need to gather people forever. You may want to try doing just one or two events and see if you enjoy it. You also have the option of joining other communities and participating. Whatever you choose, make sure it is an approach that fits your personality and objective. I personally prefer more intimate events; Tina is wildly inspired by bringing together large groups; for you it might be two or three people or even going on a hike with a friend. You should do what's right for you. To figure that out, Part

III will tackle what to do for each type of community, from social groups and business development to cause-based communities and company culture. We will also explore the differences in gathering people in person and through digital platforms, as digital has become increasingly more popular. Although all these topics might not apply to you directly, the examples can still spark ideas and give you insights.

Part III

Applying It All in Your Life

Over the course of this book I have shared a lot of examples, but I want to make sure that you feel equipped to handle any goal you might have for creating a community and connecting with people you admire. You may want to bring people together to explore ideas, or you may be building a large group of connected customers, supporters, or donors who are incredibly loyal. Although few things in life fit perfectly into groupings, for the sake of simplicity, we will explore four categories: social communities (building a friend group, hobby-driven activities, entertainment, etc.), cause-based communities (religious, social justice, support groups, etc.), business-based communities (customer development; industry specific, like all people in architecture; position specific, like CEOs from across industries, etc.), and corporate culture (having teams bond, connect, and function effectively). You will notice that no community fits perfectly into each of these categories. People come to connect around creativity at Tina's global CreativeMornings series, so is it social? Or is it business because it is for creatives to grow their knowledge and succeed? The answer is yes and yes, and it doesn't really matter. What is important is that the categories enable us to tackle ideas in an organized way.

These are the questions my team and I ask when clients ask us to design something for them, regardless of which community they would like to build:

1. Who are you looking to connect with? Their level of influence will define the connection strategy.

2. Are you looking for a single event/miniseries (the floral event, a birthday/reunion, brand launch, etc.) or to build a sense of community over the course of months/years (Red Bull Music Academy, Influencers, CreativeMornings, etc.)?

3. How many people do you want to connect with at a time? The scale should be consistent with your personality, who you want to connect with, and your objectives. Remember, the more influential the people are, the harder it is to gather large numbers of people.

4. When designing the path for the elephant and the rider, what do you want them to feel, think, and do at the end? This is where the values of the organization shine. If it isn't authentic to you or your organization, it won't accomplish what you want. Remember the peak-end rule and how we delivered flowers at the end of the Aesthetic Scentability Brunch.

5. Are these values consistent with what you care about? If you plan on running the event more than a couple of times, the values need to align with yours or you won't want to keep doing it.

6. What original format can you use that will engage this audience to produce the type of membership you are looking for? Take the time to think this through; we produce a lot of bad ideas before we get to the good ones.

7. What discovery approach will you use to have people engage with this activity?

8. Where can you further implement the Influence Equation?

9. With what we know about human behavior, will this path appeal to the rider and the elephant?

10. Is this path ethical? If a stranger knew how you designed it, would it bother them? If so, start again.

The biggest challenge will be creating a novel way to engage around your core values. In the following pages, I will share examples of how we apply this approach across business, organizational cultures, non-profits, and personal communities in order to spark your creativity and inspire you.

For additional resources, activities, and ideas, go to www.Youre Invited.info.

Chapter 17

Creating Communities
for Business Success

Very few people would consider online customer management software sexy. Yet in 2019, Salesforce estimated that they hosted more than 170,000 people at their annual conference, Dreamforce. To put that into perspective, CES, the Consumer Electronics Show, which hosts every electronics company in the world from Samsung and Sony to Microsoft and Apple, boasts just slightly more at 182,000 attendees. With billions in annual revenue, Salesforce is an incredible business success. But even though Salesforce's competitors bring in much more revenue, their annual conferences don't come close to the size of Dreamforce or the obsessive fandom of the Salesforce community. When I attended Dreamforce as an observer, at times it felt more like Comic-Con than a product conference.

So, why is it that Salesforce was able to grow such a dedicated community? The answer is MC Hammer. Yes, the award-winning early-90s hip-hop artist with baggy pants. When Hammer met Salesforce CEO Marc Benioff, he told Benioff about street teams. In the music industry, street teams cover the streets in their local city with promotions and posters to increase attention for an upcoming album or tour. That, plus meeting Reverend Billy Graham, enabled Benioff to see the power of evangelism and potential for turning customers into local promoters.

In the company's early days, Salesforce held a national bus tour and invited local customers and potential customers to come together. Benioff expected to present for a while and then field questions, but the customers were so enthusiastic that they answered for him, evangelizing the product. The customers were more interested in connecting with each other than with him. Benioff was able to stand aside and watch the community coalesce. This experience stuck, and as Salesforce grew the company made it a priority to provide opportunities for customers, enthusiasts, developers, and partners to come together.

As part of this community-first focus, Salesforce would invest heavily in ensuring people felt as welcome as possible. They design their local events so that customers can share honest feedback and testimonials, and this transparency has won over prospects. Salesforce developed an internal community team that encourages and helps organize meetups, provides support to fan groups, and even develops programming and resources to help local enthusiasts run events.

For the past twelve years, Sarah Franklin has led this Salesforce community team. Their responsibility is to ensure that the community's core values are always represented. Their mission is to have members connect, learn, have fun together, and be generous. Generous to them means giving both to each other and to the local community. At many companies, these taglines are said and forgotten, but for Franklin and her team they are requirements for everything they design, both in person and online.

The team even went so far as to create, at an incredible expense, a free online training program called Trailhead. The website provides a simple way for beginners to learn how to use the Salesforce platform and program on it. Knowing that every community member's journey is unique, they designed a number of different Trailhead paths to support people finding their way, and Salesforce has constantly refined the process. As people move through Trailheads, they earn the equivalent of merit badges for each challenge or lesson they complete, and the program has helped countless people improve their careers or start new ones. As a result, a hairdresser looking for a career change became a programmer and an unemployed father selling his plasma to buy food for his family is now a project manager who can afford family vacations.

Because Salesforce knew that learning technical skills can be intimidating without someone available to ask questions of, they built a community experience into their plan. From the moment a person registers, they are invited to participate in both the online community and a local meetup. This is an incredible level of intentionality for creating a journey and a sense of community. They have integrated their core values into a consistent community structure and journey on an international scale. With this level of design, it is no surprise they have had such incredible success engaging community influencers.

So, what does it look like when we create a business community? The answer, as always, depends on who you want to connect with and at what scale. What it doesn't look like is the traditional cold calling, hoping you will catch a potential customer just at the moment when they need your product. Instead, we develop a path and apply the Influence Equation so effectively that customers are hoping to get an invite to connect. We want them to get so much value from participating and create such deep social ties that not only does their career improve (as it did for the Salesforce community), but when the time comes that they need your services, you are the trusted source. Once you have a format down, you can consistently run it and refine it. Eventually you can launch a reunion event to bring people back together.

Since business communities can vary dramatically between industries, I recommend you define which customers fit into which influence category. For the sake of example, if you run sales or marketing for a global consultancy or accounting firm, the clients that are global influencers might be the CEOs/presidents of the largest companies in the world. Meanwhile, the industry influencers might be the C-suite or VPs and the community influencers might be the directors. You will need to categorize your customers, as titles are wildly different from industry to industry and not all people with the same title are equally influential nor do they all run the same size organizations. If you are in a nonprofit, you can use this same approach by categorizing donors and determining the best way to connect with them.

After you place your customers into influence categories, you will see how many groups you want to connect with. At large companies there could be twenty-plus programs/strategies running concurrently, as you would want your strategy to fit not only the customers' level of influence but also why they engage with the brand. A global software service provider like SAP sells so many products it is nearly impossible to track. They provide everything from accounting and HR software to supply chain and hosting service and each have a different customer. For a company like SAP, operating at such breadth and scale means they would likely want to develop separate communities for each customer group. They would have one for HR professions, a separate one for accounting, and possibly a separate one for regulated industries like government and pharmaceuticals, and so on. So, I encourage companies that have siloed products with distinct sales teams to develop their own programs but for the communities to be built on the same principles and values so there is consistency for the brand and a unified message to customers.

At this point you should have a sense of how many groups you will need to focus on (accounting, HR, supply chain, etc.) and what strategy to use for each level of influence. It may mean you have two or three communities in each group so you can connect with global, industry, and community influencers, although for most companies connecting with just industry or the community influencers is all they need. Next, you need to ask, what do we do? Rather than drown them with constant calls or emails, you need to develop an experience, either digital or in person, that will entice them to connect and foster the type of membership we want. You will test it a few times, possibly with loyal customers to get feedback, and then launch it as a consistent event series that welcomes people into the community. For an insurance salesperson, it could be a one-on-one activity over video chat, while someone selling HR services may create a community event for chief human resource officers. Once you feel you have reached a critical number, you can start hosting reunion events. Not only do these events keep you top of mind, but the more your customers or potential customers connect with one another, the closer they feel to you. You are the central hub of the community.

It often surprises people that cultivating a business community as an individual can be easier than using the resources and status of a large company. Depending on the company, people may be entrenched in a traditional corporate mindset and will have to overcome two challenges. The first is that the C-suite at large companies think they have great relationships with their "customer communities." The problem is the customers don't see it that way. They may like the salespeople, but the customers have no sense of community because they don't know each other. This severely limits the customer's connection to the brand and how top of mind the brand is. If you provide a great product, you shouldn't be worried about bringing your customers together, and yet many companies will avoid it. The second challenge is that executives tend to think their current programming works, so they don't want to change it. Let's be honest, if the status quo is their strategy at play, then it will be natural for them to get defensive when other options are suggested. The problem is that they could be spending a fortune and not getting the results they want.

It is not uncommon for global sales organizations to run thousands of events a year and spend millions of dollars courting clients. Marketers and salespeople are not scientists, so expecting them to understand human behavior would be unfair. Many strategies in the corporate world are standard practice, and if they work for you as they are, then keep following them, but if you would like a greater sense of community, know that there are steps you can take.

Fancy Dinners

When courting a customer, it is common to host a private dinner at a fancy location to draw them in or to bond after a pitch. I think dinner parties are generally a waste, even though I run a successful dinner series that has inspired other brands and agencies to start hosting dinner events with similar titles. To be clear, I doubt they were trying to copy; I didn't invent the concept of dinner or people being available to meet in the evening after work. Why none of these agencies has the longevity of the Influencers Dinner is that it isn't about the dinner; it is about the time cooking together and the game we play around the table. Given the structure of a standard business dinner, it is difficult to create lasting bonds.

The problem stems from the fact that any group of more than four or five separates into sub-conversations. Depending on the width of the table and the noise in the room, people across from each other may or may not be heard. Now you are limited to the people on your left and right. Chances are good that those two people aren't interested in each other enough to justify two hours of conversation. To add to the complexity, you will rarely be seated next to the person you want to speak to. So, it can create an uncomfortable and uninteresting experience instead of one of trust and comradery. If dinner is a requirement, consider different formats or numbers of people at a table and engineer activities that will allow them to build trust with one another. I have been to dinners where people have to switch seats every course, and others are served family style but you are not allowed to serve yourself. I once took a group on a food crawl where we visited six restaurants and enjoyed a few items from each to share. There are a lot of ways to have dinner, but it may better serve your goal to serve food in the context of another activity that promotes interaction.

Gift Giving

It may seem that I am against gift giving, as the recipient doesn't put in effort, but nothing could be further from the truth. The main issue is that almost all corporate gifts are unwanted. No one is interested in a shirt with your logo on it or another beer cozy—it's just going to end up in a trash heap. Instead, we need to be thoughtful about who we are giving the gift to, why it would be special to them, and why you and your company are sending it. I work with a done-for-you gifting agency called Giftology, started by my good friend John Ruhlin, to help me with my strategy and execution. Giftology has made everything from custom engraved kitchen knives to hand-crafted coffee mugs designed with messages from the loved ones of the recipient. As a person who runs a secret dining experience, you can see these are not only consistent with what I do, but they are high-quality cherished gifts, used often, and serve as a reminder of who I am. Gift giving is a complex topic worthy of its own book, but I recommend that you stop sending out junk that no one wants or will notice and instead consult a professional like Giftology to help you figure out what's right for your company and customers. While the wrong gifts can be a waste of budget, the right gift will capture their attention and increase trust, connection, and a sense of belonging.

Launch Parties and Large Promotional Events

These events can be a lot of fun for attendees, but they all kind of feel the same. Large space, loud music, drinks, photo booth, a few poster stands with the company logo. In 2018, I was asked to design a private product launch party for one of the biggest tech companies in the world. They were releasing a groundbreaking product and wanted something very special.

As always, I began by asking what they wanted to accomplish, with whom, how many people they wanted at the event, and what the budget was. They said $200,000 for two hundred influential people. I was dumbfounded. I didn't understand what they were planning on spending that money on. They said they wanted a famous band and top-notch food. So, I taught them the 10 percent challenge, one of the best ways to determine if you have the right budget for the event.

If they had only 10 percent of the budget, how would they accomplish the same result? At $20,000 they wanted the same party but with a DJ and slightly less impressive food. You will notice that none of their ideas connects guests to the brand and that at one tenth the budget they essentially had the same experience. In that case, why not just run this event ten times to reach more people or use the rest of the budget for other marketing efforts? So, we tried the 10 percent challenge again: at $2,000 they said they would run a fifteen-person dinner. If the dinner was designed right, the individuals attending would have more intimate conversations and connect more deeply than at a loud party. Notice, they had the budget to do a dinner one hundred times. We ran the challenge one last time. At $200, they thought they couldn't do anything, so I suggested they host a board games night and order in some cheap food. Notice that the experience that would probably be the most fun (games with cool people) cost one one-thousandth as much as their actual budget allowed for. I respect that this may not have been on brand, but it is a great test to see if you are making the best use of budget.

As we dug further into what they were hoping for, they finally told us they cared about social media posts and brand connection. This is an essential point. As a company, it is important to build around the metrics you care about. At times that metric is number of attendees or total sales; at other times it is social media posts or survey responses. Whatever it is, you have to make sure you consider it in the design of your event or your company won't want to support the initiative.

We decided to create an immersive and interactive art installation with talks by thought leaders who were experts on brand/product values. Not only did the company report that they had the biggest social media launch in their history, but in the words of one guest: "I walked in expecting a standard launch party, but people were really enjoying themselves and wanted to be there. I go to a lot of events, and you never see that. Most parties are forgettable stops in an evening." We accomplished this because we created a path for people's elephants and riders and gave them a sense of belonging. Best part was, not including our fee, we did it for $20,000 all in. The 10 percent challenge worked.

All too often, companies think they need to throw a lavish party to promote a launch, but I have rarely known launch parties to lead to significant sales or media. I understand that these types of big events might be important for company morale and culture, but we want to make sure we understand why we are gathering before we start investing heavily. Showing gratitude to the team is incredibly important, but it shouldn't be confused with marketing and sales. We need to consider how much we are willing to spend to connect with a potential customer, as the numbers often don't match the return on investment. And if you can't justify the spend, you are going to lose the budget. The point is that there are always creative solutions that can help build more meaningful connections. They may require more thinking and mental effort, but they tend to be far less expensive. Sometimes the best promotion or opportunity is a party, but you have to architect the experience to accomplish what you want. If you aren't developing a sense of community or membership, you will have to reengage people from scratch each time.

A quick story on spending: Several years ago, I was approached by a high-status hotel brand to create a celebrity summer camp. Imagine three days of camp activities taught by industry leaders (e.g., swim class led by a decorated Navy SEAL, art class by a famous photographer). Since the event involved celebrities and prominent artists, producers, musicians, and so on, it trended online thanks to coverage by *Vogue*. From the brand's perspective, even though it cost several hundred thousand dollars, the media coverage made the experience a success. From a community standpoint we could have accomplished the same level of connection at one tenth the cost. But here is the critical point: their metric for success was media, not connection or sales, and the lower cost version may or may not have met the standards for *Vogue* to write about it. So, you need to ask yourself what it's worth to have the result. If the PR value is worth it in the short run, it may make sense, but in the long run, you might want to focus more on relationships and creating novel low-cost experiences and less on the glitz and glam.

Conferences and Industry Summits

When you have a global client base and billions in revenue, an annual conference provides a phenomenal opportunity to make announcements, meet with customers, and maintain the relationship/upsell. Meanwhile, summits tend to be more midsize events with fifty to five hundred–plus people all in the same industry or role (e.g., a CMO, CFO, CIO event, oil and gas, consumer packaged goods).

I am all for these types of gatherings, as long as they are designed to connect the attendees to the brand and each other in an intentional way. Otherwise they are a lot of work and are incredibly expensive, not just financially but from a human resources perspective. The question you may want to ask is: "How can we accomplish the same business impact with far less logistics and expense?" It is like the 10 percent challenge but includes both budget and staff energy/time. You may be able to hold a small series that enables you to connect more with customers at a fraction of the cost. Hosting more people isn't necessarily better. Often you can accomplish much more connecting with a handful of people who are important to you and what you want to accomplish than having countless people walk through and barely remember you or the brand.

Celebrity Events/Meet and Greets

Brands will often hire a popular celebrity as a draw for the event to speak or perform. When the prospect arrives, the salespeople will use the opportunity to discuss the company as well. Don't get me wrong, I clearly enjoy hosting high-profile people, but potential customers will come to hear from them and hopefully get a selfie. They probably don't care about the product. Celebrities can fill a room, but you need to ask yourself: What do the celebrities have to do with your brand/product, and what are you going to do next time?

When there is no clear relationship between the celebrity and the brand, the brand loses authenticity and customers mostly learn that the brand is incredibly good at spending money. In fact, your biggest competitor can have that same celebrity speak the next week. If that's the case, there is no clear brand value. I once went to a liquor brand's party in Miami. There was an art exhibition and then a famous musician came out and sang a song about New York. Let's review: it is a liquor brand that no one associates with the arts at an art exhibition throwing a party. The brand is not known for being based in New York (in fact, they are located in a different state), and they have no association with the New York–based celebrity or her charity. The only reason I remember the brand is because the whole scenario didn't add up. Remember, our objective is to develop a deep and meaningful relationship with people by creating a path for the elephant and the rider. I'm not sure celebrity events accomplish that. Frankly, it is a lot like getting a date with someone by promising to take them to an expensive show. If they are just coming for the show, chances are the spirit of the experience and your prospects for a relationship are off.

The other not so small problem is that when you hire a celebrity, you get a big rush of attendees, but the next time you want to connect with people you'll need to get an even "better" celebrity. This means more money, and now you are competing on celebrity rather than people coming to connect and enjoy an experience that represents the brand in a meaningful way.

A side note on celebrity talent: there is a strategic difference between a surprise and a draw. If I promote a celebrity in the invitation, attendees are coming for a celebrity, but if I promote an event and there is an on-brand talent-based surprise, that demonstrates brand innovation, style, and thinking. If you use this strategy, I recommend two things. The first is to hire less famous yet incredible talent (e.g., an up-and-coming musician, magician, or performer, not David Copperfield or Taylor Swift). It can be more impressive to have access to the unknown talent. Second, you may want to switch styles—one time you have a magician, another a mixologist to teach you how to make cocktails, and so on. This way you don't have to compete with yourself.

Expert Talks/Webinars

During these events, a subject matter expert presents an idea they are famous for, such as an author on productivity or an economist on the state of the industry. I have mixed feelings about these. On one side I can clearly see a brand alignment, but on the other side it feels like the same celebrity issue—your competitor can hire them and the ideas aren't coming from the company. I would ask a few questions: In your company, is there anyone who can share a unique perspective, data, or knowledge? Is there any way to partner with the thought leader so it becomes cocreated knowledge that shares your forward-thinking approach or brand? This is also why as a speaker I create a new talk for every client. I want to make sure the client's values are shining through and that we design the right path for the audience.

Another big consideration is that the C-level executives and decision makers at a large company probably won't spend their time on a webinar. If you want to connect with them, you need to design around novelty, generosity, curation, and awe, and in most cases that means a much more intimate number of participants.

Up until this point, I've provided a lot of examples of how to deal with augmenting the current strategy, and now I want to show you what it looks like when we create from scratch.

In 2017, I was approached by one of the largest tech companies in the world. They had a few objectives, among them connecting with high-profile creators and business leaders for developing interesting collaborations. The company wanted this community to create a positive impact and inspire creativity. With this in mind, we developed a flagship event focused on creative ways to improve the world. We invited Oscar, Grammy, and Tony winners to connect with scientist, artists, museum curators, and business leaders. Twenty guests would join us after work. They were split into four groups of five and would compete to find the most creative ways to tackle global problems. It was a lot of fun, but after running it a couple of times, we realized that forced creativity around global issues was a bit much to ask after a full workday. Instead we switched the format to creative games. Among the various activities, participants were given random office materials and had to design a house, they answered trivia questions to earn points, and they were given crayons and magic markers to let their style shine. The program was a huge success, as not only did they bond with the brand and its representatives, but they learned about the company in a fun and playful way.

As relationships were built, we invited participants to pitch ideas for projects at the intersection of creativity and technology. The ideas we received were far more interesting than any pitch from a creative agency, carried more status because of the high-profile creative it came from, and caused the creative to be more dedicated to the project, since it was something they were passionate about. Think about how different this is from a creator's dinner or hiring a Grammy winner to speak on a panel.

As part of the community, their involvement is a form of self-expression, and they are opting in based on interest, not because of compensation. The community provides a true sense of belonging while developing collaborative projects that support all involved. The best part is the actual expense was minimal. The guests came to the company's office, were given art supplies, played games together, and heard a bit about the company. I honestly believe this is the future of event and community marketing.

So that you have plenty of inspiration, here are a few more examples:

- *Zero Hour:* Twenty guests arrive for dinner and are split into four tables. Thirty minutes in all their drinks are taken away and news broadcasts from South Africa are shown talking about the water shortage. Each table is told they are now a family that needs to survive. To do this they are given dirty water and told to build a filter from the supplies provided. After the activity, a conversation about the treatment of our resources is led by Winston Ibrahim, the founder of the water filtration company Hydros. This is how Hydros has built a dedicated community of customers and partners who care about the environment.

- *Fuckup Nights:* Cofounded by Leticia Gasca and Pepe Villatoro, these evenings of sharing personal stories of business failure provide participants an honest, cathartic, and often amusing experience.[1] Born of the realization that all too often people carry the shame of their business failures and never move forward, Fuckup Nights are about appreciating the attempt and learning from the process. The format of every Fuckup Night is simple: three or four people take the stage and using slides share their fuckup stories, followed by a Q&A, and ending with time to network.[2] This novel experience now runs in over 260 cities across all 6 inhabitable continents. What I love about this concept is that it takes vulnerability and celebrates it. It is a beautiful way to create a trusted and safe space for connection to develop.

- *The Thought Leaders Hike:* Once a week in San Diego's Torrey Pines State Natural Reserve, a group of authors and business leaders meet to enjoy the incredible beauty, a healthy hike, and, most important, undistracted conversation and bonding time. It all started when author John Assaraf invited friends and entrepreneurs including MDs, actors, researchers, professional athletes, and diverse talent like bestselling authors Mike Koenigs and Dr. Ken Druck to do something that would not only catalyze great friendships but also be good for their health. There are no fees to pay or initiation process; it is just a word-of-mouth get-together between trusted circles of friends and their guests. From it have been birthed countless projects, new books, businesses, and new friendships and relationships.

- *The COO Alliance:* Cameron Herold, former COO of 1–800-GOT-JUNK?, noticed that in the corporate world chief operations officers are the unsung heroes. There are plenty of events for the rest of the C-suite, but nothing for COOs. In response he launched COO Alliance, a private community for those who are second in command to the CEO. It puts the tools and systems to rapidly grow revenue, profit, and culture into the hands of people actually doing it. What makes this community so interesting isn't the format but the recognition that there are a lot of high-profile brilliant minds who would come together if provided the platform. The COO Alliance does this monthly online and quarterly in person with members across four continents and continues to grow.

• *brunchwork:* Founded by Paulina Karpis with my support, brunchwork has developed a unique business community for millennials. Every weekend, members comprised of young professionals flock to locations across the country for brunch with a twist. After some food and time for mingling, two prominent business leaders present ideas or are interviewed. The members are then split into small groups to take on a business challenge. Working together, they a develop a solution and then pitch it to the speakers for feedback. Notice that each part of the event offers a part of the SOAR model (providing skills, opportunities, access, and resources).

These examples provide a great starting point to catalyze your creativity as you consider what will bring your community together.

Chapter 18

Cause-Based Communities

———

When it comes to building a cause-based community, the two most important things to look at are membership and fundraising. Hopefully the two won't be mutually exclusive, but if you are trying to address an issue like cancer, for example, you may want to create a community of survivors or people going through treatment who support each other or you may want to fundraise to support research, help people who can't afford their medical bills, or create awareness programs.

The key here is to understand your audiences and what you are looking to do. Some organizations have one journey for their funders and another for those they care for. This could be a better strategy, as a funder's social pressures can be quite different from someone currently going through cancer treatment.

If you are looking to create a support system for patients, you may want to build your group more like a social community, the way that CreativeMornings did. This kind of community is highly organized and easily reproduceable for any community that wants to participate locally.

But what should you do if you also need to raise money and build media support? Traditional nonprofit fundraising is a by-product of a handful of high-profile donors who give a disproportionate amount, combined with what I call the gala model of fundraising. This is where the organization hosts a large black-tie event in a fancy location as a fundraiser, usually around November or December. There are a few big problems with this approach:

- *They raise a lot of money in one night:* You are probably thinking, isn't the point to raise a lot of money? And yes, you are right, but it also means that 80 percent of the entire organization's funding could come from a single night, so if it doesn't go well, they might need to fire people or close down programs.
- *The event is disconnected from nonprofit's values:* Spending $250 a plate to raise money to end hunger is frankly ironic. The organization is participating in activities not aligned with its core values and should redesign them.
- *People come for a party not a cause:* Because an event committee invites all their friends to join the celebration each year, it means that the attendees don't create a connection to the organization. As a result, every year the committee needs to work from scratch to secure guests and donors. When considering the stakes, this process is exhausting and stressful.

There are a few organizations that have started to see the writing on the wall and have shifted their approach to create deep and meaningful relationships with supporters throughout the year. The galas may never go away—after all, people love getting dressed up—but here are a few examples of what some organizations have created.

The National Multiple Sclerosis Society (NMSS) is an incredible nonprofit that supports nearly one million Americans with the disease. What makes NMSS impressive is that instead of raising most of their money from a few large donors, they bring in $200 million a year almost exclusively through grassroot efforts. When comparing that to the size of their staff and the prevalence of the disease, they punch way above their weight. The reason for their success won't surprise you: they are first and foremost phenomenal community builders.

Their initiatives have always focused on how to bring people together in interesting ways. They started programs like readathons, where children raise money for every book read, and cycling events years before others, and in the late 1980s they developed a program called the U.G.L.Y. Bartender Contest. I thought this was very clever.

Bars around the country would invite patrons to community celebrations honoring their bartender as U.G.L.Y.: Understanding Generous Lovable You. Each dollar raised counted as a single vote, and the bartender with the most votes would win U.G.L.Y.est Bartender of the Year. In Minnesota and Pennsylvania alone, NMSS would raise more than $500,000. As the negative impact of drinking became clearer, the organization phased this out and invested in a fitness-oriented strategy, growing to host more than 550 events annually. These programs include three hundred walks in communities across the country and sixty-five destination bike rides where people come together to get healthy, raise money, and enjoy the beauty of the country.

I love these programs for a few reasons. The first is that the fitness experiences give people a reason to put in effort to get healthy. They also cost the organization a fraction of a gala to produce and are easier to connect to the organizational values. This means that you can have a great experience, raise more money, and stay on mission. Developing a salon or experience-type model allows organizations to invite donors who will connect with the mission *and* other attendees. The more friends donors involve, the closer they will be to the cause. This is also where reunion and offshoot events become more valuable. If the gala is a reunion of everyone who has been participating throughout the year, it is a celebration of the community's efforts. Alternatively, offshoot events like volunteer days, trips to see the development of a project, or allowing members to host events for their friends further promote the mission while continuing to bring people together.

Since the NMSS is involved with every aspect of the disease (research, advocacy, services and programs, etc.), they have additional community-based programs for those affected by it. You can participate in one of the nearly one thousand self-help groups that meet across the country or volunteer to be an advocate for change. They have a community of thirty-three thousand engaged activists who have committed to getting attention from government officials through calling and letter writing. The big takeaway is that creating a journey or experiences for those you are looking to build support from, and for those who are affected by the issue, can lead to huge successes. This is especially true when the journey and experience is built on the values of the organization and speaks to the elephant and the rider.

NMSS has been so intentional about creating communities of supporters that they have developed original programs at every level of engagement, from those who want to stay at home and write and those who are affected by the disease or their friends and family and want to walk to those who are athletes and can ride miles on end. With this level of organization, it is no surprise they are so effective relative to their size.

Now let's talk about you and your cause. You could use a standard meeting strategy. As we learned earlier, it worked quite well for the abolitionists, but I will point out that they didn't have to compete with every cause in the world showing up on a social media newsfeed. People are now suffering from compassion fatigue. All of us are being bombarded with social issues that we are told to care about. This means to gain support, you need to stand out and focus on relationships so people's support won't just be a fad.

Begin by figuring out how many communities you are developing and then design a path for each. This means you need to know how you want people to feel when they think of your cause and what category of influence you are trying to reach. If you want to reach community influencers and apply the SOAR model, a bicycle ride is great: you can teach them skills and provide access to experts, opportunities to ride, and resources like discounted equipment through partners. Alternatively, if you are looking to engage industry influencers, make sure you develop something generous, novel, well-curated, and potentially awe-inspiring. This will be especially important if you want to connect with high-profile donors and celebrities who aren't already involved in or affected by the issue. I know that is easier said than done, but here are a few examples of what other cause-based organizations are doing:

- *GirlTrek:* What started as a social media post about taking on a walking health challenge blossomed into the largest public health and self-care program in America for Black women and girls. GirlTrek organizes hundreds of thousands of participants throughout the year for weekly community walks across America. The format couldn't be simpler: Black women and girls meet at a preset location and walk a route. These women walk because, as their cofounder, T. Morgan Dixon, points out, every day 137 Black women die of heart disease, a preventable disease that takes more lives than gun violence, smoking, and HIV combined. These women and girls walk for their health, to connect with each other, and to reclaim their streets.[1]
- *Maternal Mortality:* My team was hired to develop a program that connected philanthropists around the issue of maternal mortality. We designed the event as a private Zoom game show for five philanthropists at a time. The game was comprised of three rounds of activities ranging from trivia to tracking the number of times a ball is passed between people in a video clip. In the third and final round the host asks a question such as "How many chickens did you see in the first round of questions?" The participants are very confused, as none of them noticed any chickens, and they answer these questions incorrectly. Yet when the footage is replayed, the host points out five chickens plain as day. Each of the other guests gets similarly strange questions wrong and then a winner is announced. What follows the game is a fascinating conversation about inattentional blindness. The brain will only see what we tell it to focus on, and everything else gets ignored. So, when you are distracted with a counting game, you won't notice chickens or anything else. Which brings us to the problem of America's sky-high maternal mortality rate. Mothers' issues emerge after returning home from the hospital, and no one notices because everyone is so focused

on the newborn. It is inattentional blindness. The moment people realize what they should look out for, they can see the problem and act. It's just like the contestants—once they see the chickens, they can't be unseen. They are always aware. The beauty of this format is that it allows for a clear message about the cause to be communicated in an emotional and novel way. We can have an impact on maternal mortality issues if we just make people aware, and to do that we need your support. This is a problem we can solve through grassroots public service programming and education.

- *Alcoholics Anonymous:* Since 1935 AA has been running meetings that have saved and greatly improved the lives of millions. Their unique format of anonymity combined with open sharing creates a safe space where people can be vulnerable with their struggles. What is extraordinary is how strong a community built on anonymity really can be. They have no central authority, the meetings are independently organized, and the meetings are held in free meeting spaces. It demonstrates perfectly that you don't need money to create community; you just need to provide a platform and a format that works for the people you are looking to connect with. Thanks to the consistency, efficacy, and design of AA, people can enter a meeting in any of the approximately 180 counties and countless cities around the world and have an immediate sense of belonging and safety.

- *Barbershop Books:* Alvin Irby was shocked when the US Department of Education released a study showing that more than 85 percent of America's Black male fourth graders were not proficient in reading. In response he launched Barbershop Books, a community-based program that creates child-friendly reading spaces in barbershops and provides literacy training to barbers across America. Barbershops are a significant gathering location in Black communities, making this a brilliant strategy. According to Irby, Black men will typically see their barber once or twice a month, and each of those vis-its is an opportunity to increase boys' access to culturally rel-evant and age-appropriate children's books. What I love about this is that it works perfectly for the elephant and the rider. It catches people on their journey—they are already going to the barbershop—and allows for a small adjustment that makes a big impact.

The most effective cause-based organizations are the ones that can rally a community around an issue in a way that is consistent with the group's mission. My hope is that culturally we move away from the gala model and toward a year-round community approach sim-ilar to the National Multiple Sclerosis Society, GirlTrek, and Barber-shop Books. When a cause is integrated into a person's social circles and routines, participating and donating become a natural expres-sion of what they care about.

Next we will explore how to design the path for the elephant and the rider at your organization: whether you work at a business or a nonprofit, community culture begins within the organization.

Chapter 19

Cultivating Company Culture

———

D eveloping a strong corporate culture can mean the difference between a high-performance team and languishing in mediocrity or failing. A community approach and journey are incredibly effective for attracting and retaining the right talent and welcoming people into the team. Study after study has shown that compensation isn't the most important factor in choosing a job; people want to feel like they belong and are part of an organization with a bigger mission.[1] Sending these signals begins with the recruiting process and continues all the way through the employee experience. Culture is a topic well deserving of its own book, but the principles we talk about for connecting, building trust, and being a part of a community are just as applicable in a corporate setting as for a cause, business, or social setting. For employees, there are two journeys that feed into each other: the recruiting journey and the employee journey. All companies have a culture. The biggest question is whether you are creating it or it is developing naturally. Certain aspects may develop naturally, but if you don't guide it and ensure people have a sense of membership and belonging, it will likely have poor retention.

Recruiting		
Discovery	Engagement	Membership
How people hear about your company or position.	The processes through which people apply or are recruited.	The person being offered the position and accepting.

Although journeys are best designed from the end to the start, we will look at it in the order it would be experienced.

Company culture doesn't begin when people start working for your organization. Instead, it starts in the discovery process before people ever put in an application or are approached by a recruiter. Google has gained attention for its interesting recruiting practices; for example, a billboard with a difficult problem on it:

$$\left\{ \begin{array}{l} \text{first 10-digit prime found} \\ \text{in consecutive digits of } e \end{array} \right\} \textbf{.com}$$

The beauty of this approach is that it entices an audience who loves novel challenges to show off their skills and invest effort into the recruiting process. There are countless people with perfect resumes, but the type of person who would go home and write a computer program to solve this equation simply because they are curious is the type of person that Google wants. The billboard demonstrated the culture that Google values, and communicating about the culture begins before anybody even puts in an application. The billboard sets off a remarkable discovery process that self-selects the applicants. What journey are you putting people on when they are being recruited? Is it a job description with a list of attributes or are you inspiring people to apply with the hope of joining a community of people with similar values?

These same values need to extend to the engagement process. At one of my dinners, the CMO of a global company shared an idea related to tackling problems in the prison and criminal justice systems. This person was clearly brilliant, and as we talked, I raised a single question: "Does your company ask if a person has a criminal record on your job applications?" If you want to impact the system, start with your company. Countless companies ask the felon question, but it serves to further alienate people who were incarcerated. This is an extremely specific example, but it demonstrates an important point. We need to design the journey around what matters and do it in a way that will cause people to have a sense of membership consistent with the organization's values. The process itself either attracts or eliminates people, so it is important to evaluate everything from the design of the application and what is being asked to how people demonstrate their skills and the amount of effort they put into it. Research has shown that including people's names, genders, ages, and addresses on resumes creates a bias in our decisions. As a result, we are seeing companies redesigning the entire application process to reduce biases so that not only do they attract talent that is the best fit for the culture but also to demonstrate the type of culture and values the company holds as important.

In many industries, finding talent and being top of mind is critical. In these situations, a community-based event series for potential employees can be very useful. If you are a cybersecurity firm, hosting the monthly New York City Hackers Meetup or a capture the flag game could have the top talent come to you and stay connected.

If discovery and engagement have a well-designed journey, by the time an offer is made, people will be excited for the opportunity to be part of your company. You will notice that when done right, compensation will not be the defining characteristic that draws people to your organization. This is not to say it is unimportant, as companies that undercompensate are essentially telling their employees they aren't valued. As a result of undercompensation, these companies have less engaged staff who are not motivated to support the organization. Instead, combining fair compensation with the opportunity to be part of a culture and community that has shared values, goals, and an opportunity to grow can heavily outweigh greater pay and unappealing culture.

Once hired, they begin a new journey down the employee path.

Welcome to your first day—better yet, what activity or communication did you receive before you arrived on your first day? Did you

Employee Path		
Discovery	Engagement	Membership
The processes of being welcomed into the organization and culture	How the company connects employees and with them	The experience of loyalty and belonging to the organization

join the team for a happy hour, some ice cream, or a celebration video chat now that you are one of them? Or did you just report to a mandatory harassment training and were simply given a book about the company history? A team of researchers including Daniel M. Cable, Francesca Gino, and Bradley R. Staats were curious if mild interventions during onboarding could create significantly higher levels of retention. Despite offering incredibly competitive pay and services for employees, Wipro BPO, an Indian-based provider of telephone and chat support, was seeing turnover consistent with the industry of 50 percent to 70 percent.[2] As you can imagine, providing customer support can be incredibly stressful, not only because customers can be jerks, but also because of the pressure to sound and act more Western on calls.

In 2010, Wipro hired 605 new employees. The research team decided to test a simple change in the onboarding process. Employees were randomly split into three groups—a control group that had the standard onboarding process and two groups that had one additional hour of training and interaction.

1. *The Individual-Identity Group:* This one hour of additional training focused on the person. It included both individual work and group discussions on how they solve problems, how they describe themselves, what makes them happiest and perform best at work, and how they can bring their best self to their work group. At the end, they were given a badge and sweatshirt with their name on it.

2. *The Organizational-Identity Group:* The hour focused on "pride in their organizational affiliation and [acceptance of] the organization's norms and values." This included a discussion of Wipro's values, why the company is great, and a star performer discussing the same. Then employees reflected on what was shared and discussed it. At the end they were given a badge and sweatshirt with the company name on it.

3. *The Control Group:* This group went through onboarding in the same way Wipro traditionally did it and did not have an additional hour intervention.

When the results came in, the team was shocked. After seven months they found turnover rate in the control group was 47.2 percent higher than that of the individual-identity condition and 16.2 percent higher than that of the organizational-identity condition. Additionally, they found that turnover was 26.7 percent higher in the organizational-identity condition than in the individual-identity condition.[3]

It wasn't more money, or Ping-Pong tables, or other wild perks that made the difference. Sure, an hour about the company's values helped retention a bit, but the biggest impact was a one-hour conversation, just once, about you, what matters to you, and what you can bring to the team's success.

Whether you are creating a company culture or a community of creatives, people want to feel valued and know that they can contribute their unique skills and thinking to a role. A simple addition of an hour conversation exploring what people can add to the team signals that they are valued and have a place to grow and contribute.

If a single onboarding experience can have such a profound relationship on retaining employee talent, your company's traditions, conversations, and gathering habits clearly have a huge impact on the culture you create. Some companies thrive in a culture of radical candor, where people are obligated to share what is on their mind as long as it furthers the conversation, even if the person receiving feedback may be insulted, while other organizations develop a culture of friendly competition. Whether one is superior to another may be irrelevant. What is important is whether the culture you are trying to create is consistent with the company's values. At AB InBev, employees from all divisions are invited to see the latest marketing and advertising videos and give feedback regardless of their seniority. It allows for people to feel included and facilitates exposure and connection between people from different divisions.

You may want to ask yourself: How do I structure my company's gatherings? Is it simply an annual holiday party when people drink too much, or do you give real occasions for people to bond and work together toward a common goal? Does your company foster relationships across divisions (e.g., sales, marketing, finance, supply chain, and real estate) so they can connect? Or are they siloed, potentially leading to friction?

Creating ways of gathering within the company, in the same way that we create experiences for customers, funders, or friends, gives us the opportunity to impart and develop the company culture we want. After all, if you are not intentional with what you are creating, your employees won't have a clue as to what your company is trying to achieve. In a survey across the United States and United Kingdom by the employee engagement platform Achievers, only 39 percent of employees knew their company's mission statement and almost the same number knew the company's vision. Even worse, 61 percent of employees reported not knowing their organization's cultural values.[4] If you don't know why you are working somewhere or what you are trying to achieve, you're probably going to be confused and unmotivated. It's essential for people to know where they are going and how the culture will get them there.

At Microsoft, employee badges are embossed with the company's mission: "To empower every person and every organization on the planet to achieve more." You could ask anyone from the executive level to someone who has started that week and they'll know what the company is trying to achieve because the company's culture has been built around it.

The key here is creating a journey for the elephant and the rider that will allow employees to bond to the company and each other around those core values, culture, and mission.

Eventually everybody moves on, whether they retire or go to work for another company or start their own company. But can you create a sense of membership so strong that after people leave, they still identify with the company and maybe even want to come back? The global consulting company Kearney refers to people who have found employment elsewhere as alumni; they have taken their skills that they developed at the company and have graduated to the next stage in their career. Referring to them as alumni rather than former employees contextualizes the experience and suggests that they are always welcome back. As a result, it is quite common for alumni to hire Kearney at their new company. This kind of loyalty is not surprising for a company that is so intentional about the way they connect and the way they talk about those who have left. Regardless of what your company culture is and what values you want to impart, you may want to ask yourself how you want employees to feel about their experience when it comes time for them to move on. This can be an ideal starting point for the conversation about designing your company culture.

Chapter 20

Social Communities

———

When Keahu Kahuanui moved to Los Angeles, he thought it would be an ideal place to be part of a creative community. He pictured himself enjoying the beautiful weather, new friends, being outdoors, and working on projects that inspired him. But in a city strongly focused on image and status, he quickly realized that the friendships he formed rarely developed the depth and connection he had come to know from his community in Hawaii. Socializing tended to revolve around rehearsing lines, playing video games, or if someone had an invite, gathering for drinks at a hot new bar or party at some entertainment executive's home. While this was fun at the start, much of it felt empty. He was getting lonely, and without some intervention, he was worried that loneliness would turn into depression. Keahu ultimately desired deeper connections and closer relationships, so he asked himself a simple question: "What do I love to do that could bring people together?"

Keahu was wildly creative, so he initially thought maybe some arts and crafts meetup, but the combination of his modest apartment and being a neat freak wasn't a good mix for paint, glue, or scraps of paper everywhere. Then, while he was cleaning his closet, he looked at his incredible board game collection, and it hit him. He would invite a rotating group of six people to play games like Settlers of Catan, Risk, or Munchkin. It would let them have quality time to build meaningful relationships and hopefully leave with more than hazy memories of people's names and stories all too common from the bar scene. Not to mention, as a struggling actor on a budget, an added benefit was the low cost. People could bring their games and they could all split the cost of takeout.

Each additional board game night gave Keahu the opportunity to develop deeper bonds and to feel more at home in LA. Every time he ran the event, he would make small improvements in the experience, streamlining the process from inviting and organizing to setup and cleanup. Notice that even though he didn't have your knowledge of designing a path and the Influence Equation, he had many of the behavioral characteristics built in. There was a joint activity for the group to bond over, limited game options to reduce decision paralysis, and exciting peaks to bond them further, but more important, it served to eliminate a lot of the traditional social structures that would take away from the experience (loud music, heavy drinking, excessive focus on image). It was very clearly about fun and bonding. You will notice that great design can be just as much about eliminating distractions and unnecessary elements, as Richard did in the design of TED, as it is about adding fun or useful characteristics.

What I love about this example is that it is a beautifully simple personality-driven format for an introvert. Keahu invited people over to play board games, something that was completely outside the norm in his social circles, which made it novel and formed consistency. It developed into a culture. If he wanted to turn it into a vehicle for his career, he could have invited producers, directors, and casting agents, and if he wanted a larger place, he could have found a friend's home to host it in. But that wasn't his goal. What he wanted was to have deeper and more meaningful relationships. He wanted LA to feel like home and escape the shallow isolation it is often known for. In time, Keahu found and developed those relationships, and unsurprisingly, even though he never did it for career success, being at the heart of this community had a big impact. It turns out that a lot of the Hollywood sci-fi and fantasy actors/producers are really into board games, so an intimate and geeky night of games held at his house managed to impact every aspect of his life. Although he rarely hosts games nights these days, it served its purpose, and he now prefers taking friends mountain biking.

The key to developing a social community, as we've learned from Keahu's games nights, CreativeMornings, and the Influencers Dinner, is to pick a format you love, start with people you know or find an interested group online, and let it evolve over time, adding traditions and novelty. This approach will not only help build a community around you; it is also the perfect way to develop a habit or skill you are interested in. Getting fit is more fun when you gather your exercise-obsessed friends or join a soccer club, and reading more is easier when you are part of a book club. Ronny Chieng, the famed comedian, actor, and correspondent for *The Daily Show with Trevor Noah*, used to struggle with his weight. For years he tried to get fit by participating in activities he hated like running and weight lifting. One day he went to the local basketball court to get his mind off a recent breakup, and that's when everything changed. He joined a pickup game and had a ton of fun with a great group of people who played there every day. He realized that he was running more on the court than he ever would on a treadmill, and so he started playing daily, sometimes twice a day. In the first month alone, he lost over twenty pounds, and continued playing for years. In 2018, he decided it was time for a change; he wanted to try something new and expand his social circle. Now Ronny studies Brazilian jiujitsu and has not only made new friends and gained fighting skills, but as good as he looks in a tux, who knows, he could be playing a secret agent in the next big blockbuster.

Remember, social communities focus on activities you enjoy with people you like. You don't have to participate in them forever. Neither Ronny nor Keahu continued their initial activities, but you will notice that they always participated in some gathering or community involving joint effort built on trust and comradery. Depending on what they prioritize in their lives, they surround themselves with the people who share those values and would want to participate.

One of the design characteristics I love is using the activity as a litmus test. Similarly, the activity itself, or its description, will filter people out and ensure whoever does come has a certain perspective of the world. This is an actual ad from a newspaper placed by explorer

Ernest Shackleton to solicit men for his 1914 Imperial Trans-Antarctic Expedition:

Men wanted for hazardous journey. Low wages, bitter cold, long hours of complete darkness. Safe return doubtful. Honour and recognition in event of success.

Supposedly over five thousand people applied, and twenty-seven men signed on.[1] Although it is an extreme example, the event or activity and the way you invite people will weed out those who are not a good match. The fact that Keahu was hosting a games night weeded out people who just wanted to party at nightclubs. Not that those experiences can't be fun, but it wasn't what Keahu wanted; he wanted to create deep and meaningful relationships. Similarly, Ronny wanted to have fun getting fit. If that's not what you are interested in, chances are you wouldn't be a good fit for the pickup basketball game he participated in.

Here are a few examples of formats I really admire. You will notice how simple many of these are and how they provide a fun and novel way to gather.

- *Just One Word:* Based on Oxford University's one-word essay, where students have three hours to write about a single word (e.g., innocence, morality),[2] a small group of people are invited to bring a short story on a single word. While enjoying drinks and snacks, they each get to share their story and discover new friends.
- *The Painting:* For a novel twist on group painting, a single outline of an image is drawn across twenty-five canvases (five by five). Each canvas is given to an attendee to paint in any colors they want. The paintings are then reassembled into the large image as a beautiful collage. Each person gets to feel like they contributed while allowing people painting near each other to connect.

- *The DTLA Dinner Club:* For the past decade Josh Gray-Emmer has opened his home every summer to host twenty dinners for his local downtown LA community. The only requirement to be one of the thirty guests is you must live downtown. In the first year Josh cooked every meal, by year two his neighbors joined in, and by year three he had an idea that would take much of the burden off him. Starting with Top Chef Ilan Hall, Josh invited both prominent and new local chefs to cook for the group. The chefs donate their time, Josh reimburses them for their ingredients, and the experience is completely free to all the guests.

- *Urban Sherpas:* Every few weeks TV producer Daniel Laikind brings together a group of friends and business leaders to explore New York City. Their goal is simple: see a new part of the city and enjoy conversations. Preparation is minimal—search the internet for an activity or walk and send out emails and reminders to a group of people. Since we were outdoors and could safely distance, this was one of my few sources of in-person social interaction during the physical distancing of COVID-19.

- *Dogs of Wine:* As explained by former participant Carl Haney, new members of this under-the-radar wine enthusiast club are invited via an ominous message instructing them to show up at a restaurant at a set time. When they arrive, they are welcomed to a unique tradition. Ten times a year, the group limited to ten members would meet for great food and even better wine. The rules were: each member hosts one meal per year, members must attend all meals and are required to bring two bottles that are served blind at some point in the evening. Here is the wild part: the bottles are rated and the person with the lowest wine scores is kicked out of the group, regardless of how much the wine cost, and replaced by a new member. If a member couldn't attend, they had to send a guest, but if the guest brought bad wine or was bad company the member would be kicked out of the group. What I love about this format is that since everyone knows their time in the group is limited, the format doesn't get old. There is always a mix of familiar and new faces. People stay friends long after, but eventually everyone is kicked out, including the founder. At times when groups keep meeting as a set cohort, the experience can get stale. A format where people are rotated in and out allows for enough familiarity that it is safe and enough novelty that it is new.

- *Rental Car Rally:* It is a car race created by Franz Aliquo, but the race is not on speed but on lowest mileage as to keep people safe. Teams can earn additional points for completing tasks along the route that may destroy the car, so use a rental and max out the insurance. It is described as: "In a world filled with 'rules,' there's a midnight car rally where handsome people dress up in costumes and visit curious locations in, uh, rental cars." The winner is given some money and a gold gas pump.
- *DJ Play That Song:* It originally started as an evening where each guest brought a record and played a single track. With it they would share what that track meant to them. It has evolved a bit now that records aren't as common.

I would encourage you not to overthink this. If you want to create a social community, make a list of activities you like and invite a few friends to join you. If the experience was positive, keep doing it, improve it, add novelty, and refine the path. After a few tries, you will have a hit. As you want to expand your influence into different areas, make introductions or reach out and invite people from those areas to participate. Remember, this needs to be enjoyable or you won't want to do it, and if you find you are getting tired of a format, mix it up and try something new.

Chapter 21

Developing an Online Community

———

On Saturday, April 11, 2020, I sat in my living room dressed in a tuxedo all alone. It had been almost three weeks since the governor of New York implemented a shelter at home order due to the rapid spread of COVID-19. In that time people panicked, hoarded toilet paper, and fled the city. I realized that with so much apprehension, I had an opportunity to provide my community needed answers and a sense of stability. So, for the first time ever, we convened the Influencers online. Each session was one hour and featured a prominent thought leader speaking plus Q&A. The first one was director of the Precision Vaccines Program at Harvard Medical School, Dr. Ofer Levy (he is my oldest brother), to explain what we knew about COVID-19 at the time, and the second was famed economist Nouriel Roubini, to talk about what we can expect to happen to the global economy. Hundreds of dinner alumni attended. For a community of a few thousand, you might think it was a huge success, but as someone who cares about creating deep and meaningful bonds between people, I realized it was a lost opportunity.

Don't get me wrong, the content was exactly what people needed—answers from respected experts in a time when people didn't know who to trust. Unfortunately, I made the biggest mistake of digital events—I committed a "lift-and-shift." When most organizations design a digital event, they take their in-person experience and then stream it to their audience or customers. The problem is that their in-person event wasn't well designed to begin with, and streaming it would be an even less engaging version of the experience. This would be the equivalent of making a TV show from a book by having someone sit in front of a camera and read it to you. The content doesn't fit the medium or people's behavior.

But on this Saturday, after what I considered two false starts, I had the opportunity to do something special. This night was about giving people the chance to connect and make friends, to learn and be entertained. Since our members are spread across ten cities and three countries, it would be the first time they came together, not just for answers but as a community. It also meant that I was testing a new event design on a platform I wasn't familiar with. Up until that point I had run hundreds of dinners and a similar number of salons. I was really good at connecting an in-person audience, but designing a digital event or experience begins by throwing out everything you have ever done in person. Instead, you ask where the path needs to lead and look at how the features and limitations of the technology help you get there. If you just try to adapt what you have already done, you will get a lift-and-shift.

My team and I had met several times to try to tackle this problem. What we realized is that in-person events have at least four characteristics that we needed to provide guests if we wanted them engaged online: entertainment, knowledge, connection, and a sense of influence over the experience. For in-person events, the entertainment and knowledge are typically the main draw for large gatherings and corporate events (speaker, performer, etc.), but we often don't realize how important connection and a sense of influence are because they are almost intrinsic to in-person experiences. For example, just having someone with you, or people around, provides connection and additional entertainment (talk, share stories, etc.) and knowledge (discuss life, gossip, etc.). Additionally, at an in-person event, we have a surprising amount of influence. Even as an audience member at a show we can clap, scream, boo, dance, and impact the people around us, and at a small gathering we can interact with others. We feel like we have some influence, and we matter. Meanwhile, most digital events make us feel like we are insignificant and give us no sense of influence. We are isolated and often can't talk (we are muted) or ask questions, interact, or be heard. It is a terrible feeling, and it has become standard design.

The problems with online gatherings aren't limited to the issues with connection and having a feeling of exerting influence; they are also less entertaining than Netflix, provide little or no connection, and you probably can find the knowledge delivered more concisely on YouTube. This meant for us to hold people's attention we needed something designed to provide all four factors, and it would need to overcome people's "Zoom fatigue." Truth be told, I was nervous planning my new digital events, and it wasn't just that this was all new to me; it was also that I was only wearing the top half of my tuxedo, matched very elegantly with my Elmo pajama pants. If I had to stand, it could be embarrassing.

As attendees started to log in to our newly redesigned digital community event, I awkwardly sat there staring at the camera. At an in-person event I'm usually running around or catching up with someone, but now all eyes were on me. Not knowing what else to do, I started introducing guests to each other. Next thing I knew I had made a five-way intro among Olympians and welcomed the former director of the Centers for Disease Control. Yes, that's absolutely a not so humble brag. At the five-minute mark, we started the programming. It was originally planned as an hour and a half of content made up of fifteen-minute breakout rooms for small groups to connect and mingle and ten-minute talks. As the evening progressed, something strange happened. We were running late, and two hours in, almost everyone was still on. Three hours in, the programming had been over for a while and half of the guests were still on enjoying a giant group conversation. We realized that people were isolated and desperate to connect. If the most influential people in our culture were feeling this way, then we needed to let others join us.

Week by week, we improved and refined the process of these events. We settled on a standard format of two breakouts and four presenters, the last of which was a fun performance to ensure we ended on a good note. Talks were limited to ten minutes, as people have perspective fatigue. When you watch a show, the scene changes every few seconds, but on video chat, how long can you stare at someone's face? Since the social climate was changing rapidly, our speakers were booked only a few days ahead of time so we could tackle the most culturally relevant issues, and when appropriate, we tried to interject a bit of levity and fun so we could reduce people's stress. As a reminder, one of the four pillars of community is influence; if people don't feel like they can have an impact on the community, the community won't grow. We constantly pushed to make the experience as interactive as possible and give people a sense of influence, so we included polls and talks were followed by Q&A. We even tested different ways to make the breakouts more fun by including odd questions and activities. Legendary game designer Elan Lee of Exploding Kittens fame was kind enough to invent a game for us. One of the moments that was most gratifying was hosting several nonprofits helping frontline healthcare workers. We were joined by a deputy commissioner for the New York City Department of Health and Mental Hygiene and were able to offer support and raise thousands of dollars for rapidly delivered medical supplies. This worked so well that at every digital salon we presented a new nonprofit or two that people could support.

Week after week, guests stayed longer and longer, so we evolved. We launched "After Hours," a section where people could bring up any topic they wanted, and "Congrats," where people could share exciting news and connect with others about it. By week nine, people were staying on for more than five hours. Having given the community our goals of entertainment, knowledge, connection, and a sense of control, I would often pass the hosting privileges to a guest and go to bed. If you notice, all the principles that we talked about were built in. We looked to develop connection, trust, and community through a generous, novel, well-curated, and possibly awe-inspiring experience. To do this, we designed a path for the elephant and the rider, and in this case the path required us to throw out everything we had done before and design from scratch. It was a scary process, considering digital events were completely foreign to us, but we knew we had to adapt. We knew that the dinners and salons as we had done them had to be put on hold, and since we view community building as an infinite game, it meant that we needed to figure out how to keep playing and develop mastery in this new environment.

In the months that followed we were able to turn these learnings into concrete strategies and train many of the biggest brands in the world to apply them. Here are the basic principles I encourage you to use and a few examples to spur your creativity.

When you design digital events, never allow for a lift-and-shift; you need to design for the medium from scratch. This means considering the right mixture of entertainment, knowledge, connection, and sense of control. The risk at most companies is to confuse quantity for quality. The fact that on digital platforms hosting one thousand people costs as much as hosting five doesn't mean that you should host more. The problem is that even though knowledge and entertainment can scale to larger audiences, connection and a sense of control don't, unless the platform has the right features. So, if you want to create something that people will enjoy, the audience size should match your objectives. The more important the relationship, the more intimate the gathering should be. It will provide a greater sense of community and lets people meet and feel involved. If you want scale, it often is better to put the time and money you save on travel and event costs into increased frequency.

Another reason that scale tends to work against us digitally is that we used to be a society that enjoyed being "done to." People would sit back and watch a show or sit in an audience at a conference. We are now a society that "does." We want to be involved in the activity, and it needs to be so remarkable it is worth bragging about on social media to all our friends and followers. The benefit is that technology allows for interactivity, and some companies have figured out how to do that well, but as of writing this book, most platforms simply don't have the features to make this happen at scale.

Before we look at some examples of event formats, note that when we discuss online community building, there are a few important distinctions. Digital communities have at least three kinds of technologies they can leverage, and more coming out all the time. There are gathering technologies, which are the websites where you can find people and organize a meeting (Meetup, etc.); synchronous communities, where people are on a digital platform at the same time (Teams, Meet, FaceTime, Zoom, etc.); and asynchronous communities, where you post to a group and people can respond days or even years later (Facebook, Reddit, etc.).

Where my experience and research shine is in synchronous digital events, but I wanted to quickly touch on how important and useful the other two are. In response to the isolation many people were feeling following the tragedies of September 11, Scott Heiferman and a group of friends launched Meetup.com, a site that aims "to help people grow and achieve their goals through real-life, human connections." If you love knitting, the tech industry, reading, sports, or anything else for that matter, there is a good chance one of the 330,000 groups people started is ideal for you. With Meetup groups across 190 countries, every week over 100,000 events bring people together around shared interests. If you are a woman in Nairobi, Kenya, and want to learn about AI, Muthoni Wanyoike, the organizer of the Nairobi Women in Machine Learning and Data Science Community, can't wait for you to join.[1] If you live in NYC and love the odd British foldable bike known as the Brompton, there is a community of hundreds organized by Peter that you can ride with.[2]

When Dan, a Meetup organizer, came out as gay in 1975, it wasn't easy. Homophobia in high school led him to be bullied. You may expect that he would feel most connected to an LGBT Meetup group, but it is a food Meetup event he hosts where he feels most at home. He explains that although this group is made up of people from completely different backgrounds, "We've all been together for two years and it's changed our lives."[3]

Platforms like Meetup offer a unique way to discover active communities you can join or organize your own both in-person and online events. The important part is still designing the experience so that it brings people together around what matters to you.

While platforms like Meetup organize live interaction, almost all online community functions are built on asynchronous participation. Whether you are part of a political group on Reddit, a Facebook moms' community, a LinkedIn professional organization, or a site dedicated to pets, it is mostly built around posting and commenting. While researching this book, I came across beautiful stories of members sharing about loss or illness and people who have never met in person supporting one another. One of my favorites was a post on Reddit in 2017 asking the world to help save Christmas:

> **My brother, Max, is 25 years old and mentally about a 5-year-old. He's mentally and physically disabled and the only thing he wants for Christmas is a Blue Police Hummer [Tonka] truck, made in 2000.**

She went on to explain that it is the only toy he will play with and there are none left to buy online. Her post garnered responses from over 130,000 Redditors.[4] People from across the country offered to send her toys, and even Tonka, the toy manufacturer, joined in. By Christmas day a smiling photo of Max holding a brand-new package labeled "Max's Hummer" truck was posted to Reddit. The picture featured a thank-you note and a pile of trucks that people generously sent.[5]

Even if you are solely looking at creating in-person experiences, there is a good chance that you will want to develop some kind of digital environment for members to interact on, either to connect or as a repository for the content you have created over the years. I have scoured and researched for some best practices, and was fortunate enough to find Tim Squirrell. Tim earned his PhD studying online communities and their behaviors. He recommends a few key considerations:

- *Define your community values:* The internet can be a crazy free-for-all; if you don't have guidelines for behavior, the community can fall apart quickly.
- *Pick the right platform:* The technology you build your community on will define a lot of the interaction. Siloed communities or groups can be created on Facebook, LinkedIn, Reddit, a custom community platform, or even WhatsApp, but developing a sense of cohesion on Twitter or Instagram is near impossible.
- *Go where people are:* If you have so much clout or have such a unique value proposition that people will go out of their way to visit your site or download and use your app, it may be worth the investment, but in most cases it isn't.
- *Understand your community geography:* The more spread out people are, the more they benefit from a central online community.
- *It might be easier to join one that exists:* Much of this book examines how you can start or develop your community, but with so many already in existence, you might be able to join one that is active and thriving.

Both organizing technologies like Meetup and asynchronous platforms like social media sites provide a great way to find like-minded people, but the question remains, what do we do when we gather? In the weeks following the shelter at home order, every event shifted to video chat platforms. On a weekly basis, families hosted reunions, coworkers hosted happy hours, creatives hosted performances, and businesses tried to host digital events. As you can imagine, since my business focuses heavily on helping organizations connect in person, there was a lot of uncertainty. So, my team and I had to reinvent much of our business overnight. The digital salons provided a great education, but it was just a first step.

We knew our next goal would be to develop an original format for a specific audience, marketers. Since these professionals were struggling with the same problems we were, we hoped by coming together we could share knowledge and drum up some business at the same time.

We confirmed eight guests at a time for a video conference call. Each guest had to change their name to be displayed as a nickname when they entered. Once everyone arrived, we used the screen-sharing feature to display a trivia game we created. Each question was about one participant, and guests would use their phones to select an answer. For example:

Sara helped invent some of the most iconic products you have used. Which of these did she develop?

Yelp
the Shake Weight
the Pet Rock
the Snuggie

After all the guesses were in, the answers were revealed, points were tallied, and then Sara would introduce herself.

The objective was to demonstrate how to make digital events dynamic and entertaining while making everybody feel special with their own question. After the game, we would have a forty-five-minute conversation about what we are seeing across all industries (music, technology, sports, beauty, etc.) that we could learn from. Not only did this bond the participants and helped us learn a tremendous amount, this event series led my company to close several critical deals that kept us running during the early days of the crisis.

Notice a few elements of this experience. Yes, it has the standard characteristics of novelty, curation, etc., but it also has a great mix of entertainment, knowledge, connection, and sense of control. Any decent video chat program can share a screen, so we added fun and play to the experience while making people feel special. Aside from our salons, we generally keep digital events to an hour. It's long enough that if people show up late it still works, and not so long we lose people's attention. Could we have done a standard happy hour and had people introduce themselves and talk? Sure, but with a few minutes of effort we increased the entertainment value dramatically. We turned it from nice to fun and memorable. If you are hosting an event, consider how to insert play into the experience. There are tons of great games and even platforms that let you make your own. These games are great for providing interactivity, especially if you are hosting hundreds or even thousands of people. It gives a sense of control and can still work if you are doing a webinar.

If you are going to build your experience around knowledge, think about what exclusive information, insights, and expertise you can provide or help people understand more easily. The more uncertainty there is, the more valuable it is.

From a connection standpoint, there is often a value to put people in groups or host an event intimate enough so that everyone can participate. We noticed from the marketers' event that because people were from different industries they could speak openly. It is important to be able to vent, get advice, and be able to support one another, but if you are a competitor of someone in the room, you may need to stay quiet. If you do breakout rooms, I encourage using challenges or prompts to function as a social catalyst. One of the best I have seen was by a nonprofit known as the Creative Coalition. There were one hundred of us in the main room, and we were shown four people and told we would be put in small groups for a few minutes and had to figure out what those four people had in common. Do you know what Lenny Kravitz, Jeff Bezos, Rachel Maddow, and Betty White have in common? My team couldn't figure it out, but we had a lot of fun trying. The answer is they were all on *The Simpsons* at some point. I love that it fit their brand and was the perfect social catalyst to get us talking.

Digital events will evolve a lot over the next several years, but here are a few formats that I found were very effective and more interesting than me checking my email.

- *Theater for One:* As the name suggests, you are an attendee for a private theater experience. Although known for their in-person experience, they adapted beautifully to a digital format. You log in, and as you wait for your turn, you enjoy chatting anonymously with others in a waiting area. When your time comes, you are whisked into a live video chat. Over the next several minutes a person interacts with you by telling a story that is beautiful and inspired. The entire experience lasts less than twenty minutes and is a brilliant interactive expression of the arts.

- *Global Finance:* We were asked to design an experience that would educate influential guests about the inequalities in the global financial system and potential solutions. Without disclosing too much about the client, we created a game show where five to ten guests answered world trivia and pop culture questions, while in the process, they learned about how unfairly poorer populations are treated by money lenders. After a winner was declared, we led a conversation about the issues, potential solutions, and how they can get involved. This type of educational entertainment is highly effective, especially when the topic is cause-related.

- *Astronomical:* One of the best executed interactive entertainment experiences I have seen was a partnership called Astronomical between musician Travis Scott and the online game Fortnite. Since Fortnite is already set up to allow millions of users to interact online in groups of one hundred, they adapted the environment to allow for a fully immersive concert by Travis. It included incredible special effects and environment changes, letting users dance in front of a stage, float through space, and swim underwater, among others.

- *Escape Room:* You would imagine that being in your home alone on a computer wouldn't be a compelling environment for an escape room, but the Peters Township Public Library in Pennsylvania created a Harry Potter–themed online game that went viral. The premise was beautifully simple. Using a Google form with multiple-choice answers, they would ask people riddles; if they selected the right answer, they found the next clue to escape the room. All the questions were Harry Potter–themed and incredibly fun. What I love about this is that all the technology is free, and you can send a link to as many people as you want. An escape room or riddle challenge like this can be a great entry challenge. If people solve it, they get the link to the event, or in the event they solve it, they win some prize or status.

Regardless if you are trying to create company culture, grow a business or cause-based community, or develop the ideal social circle, you now have a thorough understanding of what influences us. You know how to build trust and connection and how to create a sense of community. Ultimately, the point of everything I have shared here is to support you and your organizations so you can thrive and enjoy higher levels of effectiveness and influence. This may be one-on-one with customers, small groups for social get-togethers, or large events for business or causes. Using this approach will make the process of creating deeper and more meaningful connections with friends, clients, and contacts not only more enjoyable but more consistent with your values and what you care about.

The next step for you is to put this to the test. Have some fun gathering people you are interested in connecting with and continue to expand from there. As you improve your experiences and grow your community, you will increase your confidence, connect with ever more influential people, and have surprising and incredible results.

Conclusion: An Invitation That Could Change Your Life

——————

At the age of ten, Daryl Davis finally had the chance to spend some time in America. Growing up with parents in the Foreign Service meant that they were moving from one country to another every two years. Being a friendly and outgoing child, he was well liked at the international schools he attended, but now he was finally home, living in the country of his birth. For the first time he could participate in the great American tradition of being a Cub Scout.

A few months in, his troop was invited to walk in a parade from Lexington to Concord to commemorate the ride of Paul Revere. Prepared with their freshly pressed uniforms and badges, the boys marched with pride down the street until out of nowhere bottles, cans, and rocks hit Daryl's head. Daryl immediately wondered, why don't those people like the Scouts? In the panic and confusion, the troop leaders surrounded him and took him to safety. As the only person in the group getting protection, he realized it was him they didn't like, but he didn't understand why, and none of the adults would tell him.

When he came home and his parents saw his injured face, he explained what had happened. His parents sat him down and explained for the first time what racism was. Growing up internationally, Daryl's classmates were all different shapes, sizes, and skin colors—with diverse backgrounds to match. He'd thought that's how every group was. Now he was the only Black person in his troop. As a ten-year-old, he couldn't wrap his brain around the idea that someone would violently hate him without knowing him. It seemed silly that anyone would care about the color of his skin, so he assumed his parents were making up this concept of racism. It wasn't until a month later when the Reverend Dr. Martin Luther King Jr. was assassinated and cities across the country were rioting that he understood that racism was real.

As Daryl grew up, he followed his passion and earned a degree in jazz. In time he had the privilege of playing blues, boogie, and rock and roll on tour with the greats like Chuck Berry. But this question "How can you hate me if you don't even know me?" never stopped bothering him.

After the release of the movie *Urban Cowboy*, the cultural demand for country music spiked, and for Daryl to work year-round, he joined an otherwise all-white country band. This meant that he was usually the only Black person in any venue he entered. One evening, after getting off stage at an all-white bar called the Silver Dollar Lounge in Frederick, Maryland, a man put his arm around Daryl's shoulder and said, "I have never heard a Black man play piano like Jerry Lee Lewis." Daryl explained that he knew Jerry Lee Lewis personally and that Jerry's style was Black in origin. Not believing Daryl but thinking him a novelty, the man invited him to sit and join him and his friend for a drink at their table. Daryl grabbed a glass of cranberry juice, and when the two toasted the man said, "This is the first time I ever had a drink with a Black man." Daryl would be the first to admit he was a bit naive to the situation and asked the man, "How can that be?"

The man looked down at the table silently, but his friend prodded him to answer, and so he explained, "Because I'm a member of the Ku Klux Klan." Daryl started laughing out loud; the man had to be kidding. After all, why would a Klansman hug him and invite him for a drink? But when the man pulled out his Klan membership card, Daryl stopped laughing immediately. The man really was a member of the white supremacist hate group. They spoke for a while longer and the man gave Daryl his number, asking to be called before the next show so he and his friends could "come to see the Black man who plays like Jerry Lee Lewis." Every six weeks Daryl would call, and the man would show up with fellow Klansmen and Klanswomen. Some would want to meet him, while others would step away. As the months passed, Daryl realized he might finally be able to get an answer to the question that had stumped him since that first Boy Scout incident: Why do people hate?

In what can probably be best described as moment of brilliant insanity, Daryl decided that he would travel the country and interview Klan members. To start it off, he asked the man from the bar for an introduction to Roger Kelly, Maryland's Grand Dragon (the Klan title for their chapter's leader of a state). Daryl never hid the fact that he was Black, but it never occurred to anyone to ask. So, when Roger showed for an interview with his personal bodyguard known as a Grand Nighthawk, they were both surprised to see their sworn enemy, a Black man, standing across from them. To Daryl's surprise, they shook hands, and after offering the men an ice-cold soda and a seat, began the interview. For three hours Daryl sat face-to-face with Roger, aided by nothing but a tape recorder and a bible. Each time the Klan leader claimed to be doing "God's work," Daryl would ask him to show the evidence.

Tensions were high, and when a sudden unknown sound startled everyone, Daryl leapt to his feet, fearing for his life, and almost attacked the Grand Dragon, assuming the Klansman had done something. Simultaneously the Grand Nighthawk went for his pistol, thinking Daryl had done something. Fortunately, they quickly realized the unknown sound was just the cans of soda shifting as the ice they were in melted. They all laughed.

Over the next years Daryl sought out Klansmen and neo-Nazis from across the country. One man he particularly wanted to meet was Bob White, another chapter's Grand Dragon and former police officer from Baltimore, Maryland. At the time he was serving four years in prison for conspiring to blow up a synagogue. Even from behind prison walls he was still active, running Klan operations at a

distance. A few years after his release, he was arrested again for assault with intent to murder two Black men with a shotgun. For this
crime, he served an additional three years. When he was released for
the second time, Daryl had the occasion to sit with him. In Daryl's
words: "The man was vehemently violent, antisemitic, racist . . . you
name it. Everything wrong with the world, it was the Blacks and the
Jews." They talked, and talked, and talked, and then talked some
more. Daryl would go out of his way to spend time with a man who
would sooner kill him than accept him as an equal. But over time,
something happened. Those brief moments of shared humanity came
through. By sheer exposure and Daryl's good nature, the two grew
closer and amazingly became best friends, and since the idea of being
friends with a Black man didn't align with the Klan doctrine, Bob
White left the Klan.

At the time of the attempted synagogue bombing, Bob was not
only part of the Klan, he was also a Baltimore city police officer. He
was an undercover Klansman who had infiltrated the police. Chances
are good that if Daryl hadn't intervened and taken the time to get
to know a man who hated him for no reason, several more tragedies would have befallen the Black and Jewish communities of Baltimore.

It has been over thirty years since Daryl's first interview, and it
turns out that on that day he discovered the answer to how people
could hate him who did not know him. When that unknown sound
went off during the interview, fear kicked in, and that uncertainty
caused both sides to react as if their lives were threatened. Daryl said,
"Not knowing what that sound was, that ignorance made us scared,
that fear led to a sudden and intense hatred, and that almost led to
destruction, either of them shooting me or me hurting them. The
core reason that those people threw the bottles and rocks at me as
a child wasn't despite not knowing me, it was because of it. Being
unknown to them led them to fear me, which led them to hate,
and then to destruction. The only solution was for people to get to
know me."

Over the last thirty years, Daryl has interviewed hundreds of Klan members. More than two hundred have left white supremacist ideology and over fifty have given him their robes, leaving a life of hate behind. It is hard to imagine the impact this has had, not only on their lives and the lives of their friends, families, and children, but also on the countless people who would have otherwise been their victims. About ten months after his first interview, Roger Kelly was promoted to Imperial Wizard (the Klan term for national leader), but Daryl never gave up on him. Year after year, they spoke and connected, and after seven years, Roger left the Klan and gave Daryl his robes.

Besides the fact that Daryl is brave beyond words, the reason I love this story so much is that it demonstrates the incredible impact of an invitation. It demonstrates that our influence is a by-product of who we are connected to, how much they trust us, and the sense of community we can foster, and that through consistency and effort, we can create unprecedented results. Daryl was able to influence these white supremacists because he found a novel way to connect through interviews, build trust through exposure and conversation, and over time, he was able to pull them in to his community. His story demonstrates that although we might feel that people are more hateful and angry than ever, it may just be that they are isolated, scared, and lonely. If the theft of the *Mona Lisa* has taught us anything, it is that the more we are exposed to something, the more it tends to appeal to us. Maybe more exposure to others will help them like us, and us like them. After all, if a Grand Dragon and Imperial Wizard from the KKK and a Black rock and roll musician can become best friends, there is no one you can't connect with.

In writing this book, I realized the shortest distance to solve any problem might be an invitation, because when someone accepts, we can create magic. The beauty of an invitation is that it has the ability to fundamentally change the dynamic. The moment someone says yes, they have committed and are stating they want to participate. When that happens, the context shifts from someone wanting them to participate to actively saying they want to engage. This is true from the moment Daryl invited a Klan member to talk, Jean Nidetch invited women to Weight Watchers, people are invited to ride with NMSS, I invite someone to an Influencers Dinner, or you invite someone to hear about your company, cause, or project.

That moment is an opening. At times you have to be brave when you make an invitation, like asking out someone you like; while other times the invite is joyful, like when you want everyone you know to celebrate with you when you two get married.

I have known no greater privilege than hosting people to cook dinner, clean floors, and wash dishes together. In the process, not only do we develop deep and meaningful relationships that will last a lifetime, but we have a positive impact by raising money for causes, bringing awareness to issues, and supporting one another. All of this started with a single invite to a group of friends.

So now I have an invitation for you.

You are cordially invited to participate in a life-changing experience. At no point in modern history have people been more isolated, lonely, and disconnected. Unsurprisingly, this affects people regardless of income and success. Now you have all the tools and knowledge to connect with them, build trust, and create a sense of community. In the process, you will have the privilege of being happier, more fulfilled, and healthier, you will find more success in your career, help the causes you care about, positively impact the lives of your loved ones, and almost anything else that is important to you.

You may be curious about who will take the journey with you, and the answer is anyone you want. It just might take some time.

You probably won't apply all the ideas in this book, so all I ask is that you reach out to someone, or a few people, or a few hundred people, and find something to connect about and then keep doing it. Whatever you do, make it your own, with your own traditions, activities, and sayings so it lives with your values.

Please let me know if you accept. An incredible life awaits, and it all begins with an invitation.

Sincerely yours,
Jon Levy
Founder and Host
The Influencers

PS: I can't wait to hear about the journey you create, both for yourself and for people's elephants and riders.

Acknowledgments

How on earth am I going to be able to acknowledge everybody who supported me through this process?

Well, I know I don't need to thank Hollis Heimbouch for working with me hour after hour to refine this idea, and even brilliantly selecting the title of this book, because she knows how awesome she is. Clearly, someone so accomplished and successful doesn't need to hear from me that she has the incredible skill of balancing her commitment to a great product and compassion for those working on it. Similarly, Rebecca Raskin is likely aware of how appreciative I am for all of the random panicked phone calls, quick turnarounds and edits, advice, insight, and expertise in the publishing process. By now she is aware that I am appreciative to have had her as an editor, especially when she stuck to her guns and wouldn't let me get away with a less than absolutely clear explanation of the concepts. I certainly don't need to express appreciation for her sweet demeanor throughout the months of writing during a pandemic. As such it is completely unnecessary to point out that both Hollis Heimbouch and Rebecca Raskin have names that sound like secret identities of Marvel comic book characters, but they are also real-life heroines.

So rather than waste my time saying all those things they already know, I will just say, "You rock!" and I think they will read between the lines.

The truth is I wouldn't have written this book if it wasn't for the incredible patience and good nature of my agent Jim Levine. Far before the time I met him, I was hearing rumors of a mensch that is like no other book agent on the planet. Thank you for working with me, proposal after proposal, until we found something we loved. I was introduced to Jim through a dinner alumnus. I love this person like a brother, and getting to meet him and become friends has been an incredible honor. Thank you, Shane Snow! The impact your invitation to meet Jim has had on my life is amazing. I look forward to many more years of friendship, shenanigans, tomfoolery, and ballyhoo.

Let's be honest, you probably didn't pick up this book for my ideas; if anything it was for Rodrigo Corral's incredible design work. It takes a lot of talent to take a complex idea and boil it down to a simple and fun format. Thank you, Rodrigo, for bringing my words to life in such a fun way.

Dasha, my incredible wife. Thank you for all of your support through this process. I apologize that my book is not an incredible piece of historical fiction, or about cats, which I know you would have enjoyed much more. I know you are probably tired of hearing my stories over and over again, but thank you for helping edit and providing critical feedback. I look forward to seventy-seven more years together. I love you.

Mary Spehar, or should I say Codi, as the world knows you. I would have never been able to have gotten this book done if I didn't have someone as reliable and good-hearted to make sure the logistics for the Influencers Community were taken care of. Thank you for your years of commitment to bringing people together.

To bring this book to life, I interviewed and connected with countless people. In chapter order so I don't play favorites: Paul Touro, Dr. Manisha Sinha, Dr. David Burkus, Kaj Larsen, Dr. Sharon Levy, Dr. Kent Grayson, William Nadeau, Vinny Green, John Roulin, Gino Leocadi, Dr. Jeffrey Polzer, Dr. Paul J. Zak, Iggy Ignatius, Dr. Moran Cerf, Scott Sanders, Allen Gannett, Torsten Schmidt, Many Ameri, Richard Millington, Ryan Verschoor, Rob Fleming, Coss Marte, Gareb Shamus, Jeff Davis, Todd Martens, Scott Rogers, Josh Shipley, Valorie Kondos, Mary Pilon, Tina Roth-Eisenberg, Simon Mulcahy, Stephanie Buscemi, Sarah Franklin, Suzanne DiBianca, Cameron Herold, Mike Koenigs, Paulina Karpis, John Scott, Enver Gjokaj, Alvin Irby, Julie Gerberding, Jodi Harris, Keahu Kahuanui, Josh Gray-Emmer, Daniel Laikind, Carlos Haney, Franz Aliquo, David Siegel, Christopher Slowe, Tim Squirrell, Christine Moellenberndt, Daryl Davis, Elysa Mardin, Brian Collins, Apollo Robbins, and Carsten de Dreu.

Since I can thank anyone I want here, and no one can stop me, I will take a moment to mention my entire family so they can see their names in print. In age order: Benjamin, Hanna, Ofer, Bat-Sheva, Amnon, Orly, Nahuel, Isaiah, Aydin, Emmanuel, and Starfire. You may have noticed, aside from my parents, I am really the only person in the family who has a normal name. And, of course, my wife's side of the family: Gosha, Vladimir, Rimma, Albina, Viktor, Anzhela, Semyon (aka Simchiki), and Salem.

Thank you, feedback squad: Daniel Laikind, Liam Alexander, Ryan Bethea, Zoe Papalaskaris, and Brian Collins, who I depended on for insight and advice throughout the process. I also want to thank Eric Maskin, Nathan Adrian, Iliza Shlesinger, Nia Vardalos, and Jesse Carmichael, who were good enough to take the time to give me a quote for the book.

And, of course, the rest of the HarperCollins team, Brian Perrin and Laura Cole from marketing, Leslie Cohen from publicity, and Jocelyn Larnick from production. Writing a book is just part of the process; helping make it a success is an incredible journey and I will never be able to acknowledge everyone, but I do want to say thank you to Bracken Darrell, Beth Galetti, Craig Clemens, Sarah Anne Stewart, Christy Pambianchi, Abby Klanecky, Ajay Kori, Alan Schaaf, Alex Liu, Amy Doescher, Andrea Sullivan, Anjali Sud, Anne Clarke Wolff, Ariel Charytan, Daniel Binns, Camille Bidermann, Carleigh Jaques, Carrie Davis, Charlotte Van Reyk, Chieh Huang, Chris Slowe, Chris Walther, Christopher Walker, Christopher Walther, Craig Forman, Daniel O'Brien, Danielle Weinblatt, David Jaffe, David Messinger, David Siegel, Doug Dawson, Eric Brewer, Eric Dunn, Fran Della Badia, Frank Longobardi, Jacquelyn Caglia, Jason Baer, Jennifer Henry, Jim Brady, Jodi Arden, Jodi Harris, Joe Belfiore, Johann Wrede, Julie Gerberding, Kate Johnson, Katie Loeb, Katrina Klier, Kevin King, Laura Barr, Margaret Lazo, Marvin Krislov, Olga Osminkina, Pamela Liebman, Patrick Srail, Paul Fabretti, Phil Keslin, Robbie Meyers,

Robert Hanson, Shauna Sweeney, Simon Mulcahy, Steve Clayton, Suki Sandhu, Susan Gaffney, Suzanne DiBianca, Howard Upchurch, J. Allen Brack, Jim Wagner, John Hagel, Joyce Green, Katie Loeb, Kristina Libby, Laura Barr, Margaret Lazo, Marissa Andrada, Mauro Porcini, Mick McConnell, Neil Lindsay, Nicole Clemens, Nicolas Cole, Siddharth Taparia, Steve Clayton, Suchit Dash, Sylvia Zhou, Vicki Walia, Zach Overton, and the countless people who I didn't have a chance to add to the list before the book went to print.

Last, I want to acknowledge all the thousands of people who accepted my invitations over the years. You may have come for a great meal with decent company, but we all got the exact opposite. This book has been shaped in every way by the conversations we shared. Thank you.

Notes

Chapter 1: The Power of an Invitation

1. "Frederick Douglass / My Escape from Slavery Audiobook," YouTube, July 23, 2014. https://www.youtube.com/watch?v=jGi9jtS7MKc.
2. Frederick Douglass (n.d.)., retrieved August 8, 2020, from https://www.pbs.org/wgbh/aia/part4/4p1539.html.
3. "10 Facts on Obesity," World Health Organization, October 16, 2017. https://www.who.int/features/factfiles/obesity/en.
4. Marisa Meltzer, *This Is Big: How the Founder of Weight Watchers Changed the World (and Me)* (London: Chatto & Windus, 2020).
5. Robert J. Cole, "H. J. Heinz to Buy Weight Watchers For $71 Million," May 5, 1978. https://www.nytimes.com/1978/05/05/archives/hj-heinz-to-buy-weight-watchers-for-71-million-hj-heinz-agrees-to.html.
6. Nicholas A. Christakis and James H. Fowler, "The Spread of Obesity in a Large Social Network over 32 Years," *New England Journal of Medicine* 357 (July 2007): 370–379, https://www.nejm.org/doi/full/10.1056/NEJMsa066082.
7. Manisha Sinha, *The Slave's Cause: A History of Abolition* (New Haven, CT: Yale University Press, 2016).
8. Sinha, *The Slave's Cause*.
9. DeNeen L. Brown, "Frederick Douglass Needed to See Lincoln. Would the President Meet with a Former Slave?" *Washington Post*, February 14, 2018. https://www.washingtonpost.com/news/retropolis/wp/2018/02/14/frederick-douglass-needed-to-see-lincoln-would-the-president-meet-with-a-former-slave.
10. Tiziana Casciaro, Francesca Gino, and Maryam Kouchaki, "The Contaminating Effects of Building Instrumental Ties: How Networking Can Make Us Feel Dirty," *Administrative Science Quarterly*, October 6, 2014. https://journals.sagepub.com/doi/10.1177/0001839214554990.
11. Casciaro, Gino, and Kouchaki, "The Contaminating Effects of Building Instrumental Ties."

Chapter 2: The Benefit of Belonging

1. "Thirty Years of America's Drug War," *Drug Wars / Frontline*. Accessed August 8, 2020. https://www.pbs.org/wgbh/pages/frontline/shows/drugs/cron/index.html.
2. "Interview, Dr. Jerome Jaffe," *Drug Wars / Frontline*." Accessed August 8, 2020. https://www.pbs.org/wgbh/pages/frontline/shows/drugs/interviews/jaffe.html.
3. Harsh Chalana et al., "Predictors of Relapse after Inpatient Opioid Detoxification during 1-Year Follow-Up," *Journal of Addiction*, September 18, 2016. https://www.ncbi.nlm.nih.gov/pmc/articles/PMC5046044.
4. "Bruce Alexander—Dislocation Theory of Addiction," YouTube, July 26, 2018. https://www.youtube.com/watch?v=05FPW4vwinA.

5. Bruce Alexander, "Treatment for Addiction: Why Aren't We Doing Better?" May 28, 2018. https://www.brucekalexander.com/articles-speeches/treatment arecovery/295-treatment-for-addiction.

6. Anne Christensen et al., "Significantly Increased Risk of All-Cause Mortality among Cardiac Patients Feeling Lonely," *BMJ Journals Heart*, January 1, 2020. https://heart.bmj.com/content/106/2/140.abstract.

7. Jamie Ballard, "Millennials Are the Loneliest Generation," YouGov, July 30, 2019. https://today.yougov.com/topics/lifestyle/articles-reports/2019/07/30/loneliness -friendship-new-friends-poll-survey.

8. Miller McPherson, Lynn Smith-Lovin, and Matthew E. Brashears, "Social Isolation in America: Changes in Core Discussion Networks over Two Decades," *American Sociological Review* 71, no. 3 (2006): 353–75. Accessed August 12, 2020. www .jstor.org/stable/30038995.

9. Susan Pinker, *The Village Effect: How Face-to-Face Contact Can Make Us Healthier and Happier* (Toronto: Vintage Canada, 2015).

10. Susan Pinker, "Transcript of 'The Secret to Living Longer May Be Your Social Life,'" TED, April 2017. https://www.ted.com/talks/susan_pinker_the_secret _to_living_longer_may_be_your_social_life/transcript?language=en.

11. Julianne Holt-Lunstad, Timothy B. Smith, and J. Bradley Layton, "Social Relationships and Mortality Risk: A Meta-Analytic Review," *PLOS Medicine*, July 27, 2010. https://journals.plos.org/plosmedicine/article?id=10.1371%2Fjournal .pmed.1000316; Lisa F. Berkman et al., "Social Integration and Mortality: A Prospective Study of French Employees of Electricity of France—Gas of France: The GAZEL Cohort," *American Journal of Epidemiology*, January 15, 2004. https:// academic.oup.com/aje/article/159/2/167/166374.

Chapter 3: What Trust Is Made Of

1. Jonathan B. Freeman et al., "Amygdala Responsivity to High-Level Social Information from Unseen Faces," *Journal of Neuroscience*, August 6, 2014. https://www .jneurosci.org/content/34/32/10573.abstract.

2. New York University, "Changing Faces: We Can Look More Trustworthy, but Not More Competent," *ScienceDaily*. Accessed August 12, 2020. www.sciencedaily .com/releases/2015/06/150618121655.htm.

3. Karel Kleisner et al., "Trustworthy-Looking Face Meets Brown Eyes," *PLOS One*, January 9, 2013. https://journals.plos.org/plosone/article?id=10.1371%2Fjournal .pone.0053285.

4. Casey A. Klofstad, Rindy C. Anderson, and Susan Peters, "Sounds like a Winner: Voice Pitch Influences Perception of Leadership Capacity in Both Men and Women," *Proceedings of the Royal Society B*, March 14, 2012. https://royalsociety publishing.org/doi/full/10.1098/rspb.2012.0311.

Chapter 4: The Science of Building Trust Quickly, aka Why Everyone Loves a Dombås

1. "Download Special Report: The State of Consumer Trust," Morning Consult, April 12, 2020. https://morningconsult.com/form/most-trusted-brands-report -download.

2. Kurt Badenhausen, "How Michael Jordan Will Make $145 Million In 2019," *Forbes*, August 28, 2019. https://www.forbes.com/sites/kurtbadenhausen/2019/08/28/how-michael-jordan-will-make-145-million-in-2019.

3. Smriti Bhagat et al., "Three and a Half Degrees of Separation," Facebook Research, February 4, 2016. https://research.fb.com/blog/2016/02/three-and-a-half-degrees-of-separation.

4. Peter Applebome, "At a Campus Scarred by Hazing, Cries for Help," *New York Times*, September 18, 2012. https://www.nytimes.com/2012/09/19/nyregion/amid-hazing-at-binghamton-university-cries-for-help.html.

5. "The Mawé Tribe Subject Themselves to over 120 Bullet Ant Stings | Wildest Latin America," YouTube, Discovery UK, August 3, 2018. https://www.youtube.com/watch?v=Cb5BK2NMAwU.

6. "Wearing a Glove of Venomous Ants," *National Geographic*, YouTube, March 3, 2011. https://www.youtube.com/watch?v=XEWmynRcEEQ.

7. Vilma Pinchi et al., "Dental Ritual Mutilations and Forensic Odontologist Practice: A Review of the Literature," *Acta Stomatologica Croatica*, March 2015. https://www.ncbi.nlm.nih.gov/pmc/articles/PMC4945341.

8. Steven Shaw, "Matis Hunting Trials," *AskMen*. Accessed August 11, 2020. https://www.askmen.com/top_10/entertainment/top-10-male-initiation-rituals_3.html.

9. "Bruce's First Matis Ritual," BBC Studios, Bruce Parry, YouTube, June 8, 2017. https://www.youtube.com/watch?reload=9&v=AuWAkt31BV8.

Chapter 5: The Problem with Connecting

1. Jon Levy, Devin Markell, and Moran Cerf, "Polar Similars: Using Massive Mobile Dating Data to Predict Synchronization and Similarity in Dating Preferences," *Frontiers in Psychology*, September 6, 2019. https://www.frontiersin.org/articles/10.3389/fpsyg.2019.02010/full?report=reader.

2. Brett W. Pelham, Matthew C. Mirenberg, and John T. Jones, "Why Susie Sells Seashells by the Seashore: Implicit Egotism and Major Life Decisions," *Journal of Personality and Social Psychology* 82, no. 4 (2002): 469. https://pubmed.ncbi.nlm.nih.gov/11999918/.

3. Jonah Berger et al., "From Karen to Katie: Using Baby Names to Understand Cultural Evolution," *Psychological Science* 23, no. 10 (2012): 1067–73. https://journals.sagepub.com/doi/10.1177/0956797612443371.

4. "The Missing Piece: Mona Lisa, Her Thief, the True Story," IMDb.com, October 20, 2012. https://www.imdb.com/title/tt1816681.

5. Noah Charney, "Pablo Picasso, Art Thief: The 'Affaire des Statuettes' and Its Role in the Foundation of Modernist Painting," *Arte, Individuo y Sociedad* 26, no. 2 (2014): 187–198.

6. James Zug, "Stolen: How the Mona Lisa Became the World's Most Famous Painting," *Smithsonian Magazine*, June 15, 2011. https://www.smithsonianmag.com/arts-culture/stolen-how-the-mona-lisa-became-the-worlds-most-famous-painting-16406234.

7. Zug, "Stolen."

8. NPR staff, "The Theft That Made The 'Mona Lisa' A Masterpiece," NPR. Ac-

cessed August 12, 2020. https://www.npr.org/2011/07/30/138800110/the-theft
-that-made-the-mona-lisa-a-masterpiece.

9. Thomas Allen and Gunter Henn, *The Organization and Architecture of Innovation* (Burlington, MA: Elsevier, 2007).

Chapter 7: Connecting with Global and Industry Influencers

1. Jim Dobson, "Billionaire Summer Camp: The Rich and Famous Flock to Sicily for the 7th Annual Google Retreat," *Forbes*, July 30, 2019. https://www.forbes.com/sites/jimdobson/2019/07/30/billionaire-summer-camp-the-rich-and-famous-flock-to-sicily-for-the-7th-annual-google-retreat.

2. "About Bilderberg Meetings," Homepage. Accessed August 13, 2020. https://bilderbergmeetings.org/index.html.

3. Silvia Amaro, "Here's Who's Going to Davos This Year," CNBC, January 14, 2020. https://www.cnbc.com/2020/01/14/wef-2020-heres-who-is-going-to-davos-this-year.html.

4. Leah Binkovitz, "Why TED Founder Richard Saul Wurman Thinks TED Is So Last Century," *Smithsonian Magazine*, July 16, 2012. https://www.smithsonianmag.com/smithsonian-institution/why-ted-founder-richard-saul-wurman-thinks-ted-is-so-last-century-2549699.

5. "History of TED," TED. Accessed August 13, 2020. https://www.ted.com/about/our-organization/history-of-ted.

6. "History of TED."

7. "Conversation with Richard Saul Wurman 'One Way': Richard Saul Wurman at TEDxGrandRapids," YouTube, TEDx Talks, June 16, 2014. https://www.youtube.com/watch?v=ec-ENp5P0A0; Binkovitz, "Why TED Founder Richard Saul Wurman Thinks TED Is So Last Century."

8. Bob Tedeschi, "Giving Away Information, but Increasing Revenue," *New York Times*, April 16, 2007. https://www.nytimes.com/2007/04/16/technology/16ecom.html?_r=1.

9. Nico Bunzeck and Emrah Düzel, "Absolute Coding of Stimulus Novelty in the Human Substantia Nigra/VTA," *Neuron*, U.S. National Library of Medicine, August 3, 2006. https://pubmed.ncbi.nlm.nih.gov/16880131.

10. Dan Campbell, *Six-Word Memoirs* (Baltimore: America Star Books, 2011).

11. "Awe," WordReference.com, 2020. https://www.wordreference.com/definition/awe.

Chapter 8: Connecting with Community and Personal Influencers

1. Tibor Krausz, "The Red Bull Story: How World's Top Energy Drink Began in Thailand, but It Took an Austrian to Make It a Global Phenomenon," *South China Morning Post*, July 28, 2018. https://www.scmp.com/lifestyle/food-drink/article/2156996/red-bull-story-how-worlds-top-energy-drink-began-thailand-it.

2. THR staff, "Pepsi Revives Michael Jackson in Marketing Campaign," *Hollywood Reporter*, May 4, 2012. https://www.hollywoodreporter.com/news/pepsi-revives-michael-jackson-marketing-320347.

3. "Giving Wings to People and Ideas," Red Bull Energy Drink, Red Bull NZ. Ac-

cessed August 13, 2020. https://www.redbull.com/nz-en/energydrink/company
-profile.
4.   Ed Gillett, "What Does Red Bull's Corporate Exit Mean for Underground Music?" *Quietus*, April 4, 2019. https://thequietus.com/articles/26290-red-bull-music
-academy-closing-electronic-music.

Chapter 9: The Structure of Community

1.   David W. McMillan and David M. Chavis, "Sense of Community: A Definition
and Theory," *Journal of Community Psychology* 14, no. 1 (1986): 6–23.
2.   Pinker, "Transcript of 'The Secret to Living Longer May Be Your Social Life.'"
3.   McMillan and Chavis, "Sense of Community: A Definition and Theory."

Chapter 10: Membership

1.   "Kamp Staaldraad," Wikipedia. Accessed February 12, 2020. https://en.wikipedia
.org/wiki/Kamp_Staaldraad.
2.   "10 of the Biggest Scandals in Rugby History," *Ruck*, December 16, 2019. https://
www.ruck.co.uk/eight-of-the-biggest-scandals-in-rugby-history.
3.   "List of Rugby Union Test Caps Leaders," Wikipedia. Accessed June 18, 2020.
https://en.wikipedia.org/wiki/List_of_rugby_union_test_caps_leaders.
4.   "ARU Admit Defeat in Bok Row," Internet Archive: Wayback Machine, June 27,
2007. https://web.archive.org/web/20070629225151/http:/www.news24.com/News
24/Sport/Rugby/0,2-9-838_2137111,00.html.
5.   Paul Rees, "Rugby World Cup: South Africa 37–20 Fiji," *Guardian*, October 8, 2007.

Chapter 11: Influence

1.   Kevin Morris, "Wikipedians Wage War over Capital 'I' in New *Star Trek* Film,"
Daily Dot, March 3, 2020. https://www.dailydot.com/society/wikipedia-star-trek
-into-darkness-capitalization.
2.   "Talk: Star Trek into Darkness," Wikipedia. Accessed October 19, 2015. https://
en.wikipedia.org/w/index.php?title=Talk%3AStar_Trek_into_Darkness.
3.   Joel Cunningham, "5 Great Books Too Short for NaNoWriMo," Barnes & Noble
Reads, December 4, 2013. https://www.barnesandnoble.com/blog/5-great-books
-too-short-for-nanowrimo.

Chapter 13: Shared Emotional Connection

1.   "Google Books Ngram Viewer," Google Books. Accessed August 13, 2020. https://
books.google.com/ngrams/graph?content=cosplay.

Chapter 14: What Is a Path and How Will It Change Your Life?

1.   Anthony Cuthbertson, "This Google AI Can Predict When You'll Die," *Independent*,
June 19, 2018. https://www.independent.co.uk/life-style/gadgets-and-tech/news
/google-ai-predict-when-die-death-date-medical-brain-deepmind-a8405826
.html.
2.   Brent Snook et al., "Taking Stock of Criminal Profiling: A Narrative Review and
Meta-Analysis," *Criminal Justice and Behavior* 34, no. 4 (April 2007): 437–53.

3. Samuel Stebbins, "What's the Average Annual Income after Taxes in Every State?" *USA Today*, June 27, 2019. https://eu.usatoday.com/story/money/2019/06/01/how-much-the-average-income-nets-you-after-taxes-in-every-state/39530627.
4. "The Importance of Irrelevant Alternatives," *Economist*, May 22, 2009. https://www.economist.com/democracy-in-america/2009/05/22/the-importance-of-irrelevant-alternatives.

Chapter 15: Designing a Path

1. Valorie Kondos Field, "Transcript of 'Why Winning Doesn't Always Equal Success,'" TED, December 2019. https://www.ted.com/talks/valorie_kondos_field_why_winning_doesn_t_always_equal_success/transcript.
2. Field, "Transcript of 'Why Winning Doesn't Always Equal Success.'"

Chapter 16: Your Path for Creating Community

1. "Re:Work," Google. Accessed August 13, 2020. https://rework.withgoogle.com/print/guides/5721312655835136.

Chapter 17: Creating Communities for Business Success

1. Leticia Gasca, "Leticia Gasca," TED. Accessed October 29, 2020. https://www.ted.com/speakers/leticia_gasca.
2. "Jakarta," Fuckup Nights, April 23, 2019. https://www.fuckupnights.com/jakarta.

Chapter 18: Cause-Based Communities

1. T. Morgan Dixon and Vanessa Garrison, "Transcript of 'The Trauma of Systematic Racism Is Killing Black Women. A First Step toward Change . . . ,'" TED, April 2017. https://www.ted.com/talks/t_morgan_dixon_and_vanessa_garrison_the_trauma_of_systematic_racism_is_killing_black_women_a_first_step_toward_change/transcript?language=en.

Chapter 19: Cultivating Company Culture

1. Barry Schwartz, *Why We Work* (New York: Simon and Schuster, 2015).
2. Dan Cable, Francesca Gino, and Bradley Staats, "The Powerful Way Onboarding Can Encourage Authenticity," *Harvard Business Review*, November 26, 2015. https://hbr.org/2015/11/the-powerful-way-onboarding-can-encourage-authenticity.
3. Daniel M. Cable, Francesca Gino, and Bradley R. Staats, "Breaking Them in or Eliciting Their Best? Reframing Socialization around Newcomers' Authentic Self-Expression," *Administrative Science Quarterly* 58, no. 1 (2013): 1–36.
4. "Many Employees in North America and The United Kingdom Are Not Happy at Work, According to Achievers' Latest Study," *Achievers*. Accessed August 13, 2020. https://www.achievers.com/press/many-employees-north-america-and-united-kingdom-are-not-happy-work-according-achievers-latest.

Chapter 20: Social Communities

1. Time staff, "The Greatest Adventures of All Time: Ernest Shackleton," *Time*, September 12, 2003. http://content.time.com/time/specials/packages/article/0,28804,1981290_1981354_1981610,00.html.

2. Jessica Shepherd, "The Word on Oxford University's All Souls Fellows Exam Is: Axed," *Guardian*, May 14, 2010. https://www.theguardian.com/education/2010/may/14/oxford-university-all-souls-college-exam.

Chapter 21: Developing an Online Community

1. Meetup, "Nairobi Women in Machine Learning and Data Science," Facebook Watch, November 13, 2018. https://www.facebook.com/meetup/videos/2005513662878690/?d=n.
2. Meetup, "Meet Peter—Brompton Bicycle NYC," Facebook Watch, November 24, 2018. https://www.facebook.com/meetup/videos/204534770354004/?d=n.
3. Meetup, "Meetup Group Story-Food," Facebook Watch, February 17, 2018. https://www.facebook.com/meetup/videos/10156178785234588/?d=n.
4. r/pics, "Every Christmas, I Have to Buy the Exact Same Toy Truck for My Brother," Reddit. Accessed August 13, 2020. https://www.reddit.com/r/pics/comments/7gdfvm/every_christmas_i_have_to_buy_the_exact_same_toy.
5. r/pics, "Thanks to Reddit, Max Got His New Hummer Truck for Christmas!" Reddit. Accessed August 13, 2020. https://www.reddit.com/r/pics/comments/7m2ey7/thanks_to_reddit_max_got_his_new_hummer_truck_for.

Index

About the Author

————

JON LEVY is a behavioral scientist best known for his work in influence, human connection, and decision-making. He specializes in applying the latest research to transform the ways companies approach marketing, sales, consumer engagement, and culture. His clients range from Fortune 500 brands like Microsoft, Google, AB InBev, and Samsung to startups.

More than a decade ago, Jon founded The Influencers Dinner, a secret dining experience for industry leaders from Nobel laureates, Olympians, celebrities, and executives to artists, musicians, and the Grammy-winning voice of the bark from "Who Let the Dogs Out." Guests cook dinner together but can't discuss their careers or give their last names. Once seated to eat, they reveal who they are. Over time, these dinners developed into a community. With thousands of members, The Influencers is the largest community of its type worldwide.

In his free time, Jon works on outrageous projects, among them spending a year traveling to all seven continents and attending the world's greatest events (Grand Prix, Art Basel, Burning Man, Running of the Bulls, etc.), barely surviving to tell the tale. These adventures were chronicled in his first book, *The 2 AM Principle: Discover the Science of Adventure*.